SATAN HAS BLUE EYES

(a love story)

Robin Peterson

Satan Has Blue Eyes

Copyright @2021
by Robin Peterson TXU2259430

ISBN: 979-8-9875486-0-8 (Paperback)
ISBN: 979-8-9875486-1-5 (Hardcover)
ISBN: 979-8-9875486-2-2 (eBook)

Lovingly dedicated to Zoey and all her
wonderful adventures to come…

Acknowledgements

I want to start by thanking my amazing mother who didn't just tell me but showed me by example how to be a strong woman. To be a free thinker, how to be inwardly powerful while she supported me unconditionally with her love. My two sons who brought a different level of growth and love into my life.

As you read this book you will understand my gratitude for the many strangers that miraculously seemed to show up out of know where, making sure I was protected and had safe passage. While risking their own lives.

It's a debt I will never be able to repay, may your lives reflect your kindness.

Through the process of writing this book there were many people that helped me along the path. My gift-ed editor Jasmyne Boswell who gave me the guidance and confidence to tell the story of Satan Has Blue Eyes. Members of my critique group, Helen Kritzler, Connie Moresco Leach, Susan Bradford and Milda Vaivada, just a few, whose supportive insight was invaluable.

Special thanks to Eve Rose, Madeleine Swart and dear Tricia Tellier for your kind eyes and reading expertise.

I have come to believe these people didn't just show up in my life and this book doesn't just show up in yours. Some call it fate, serendipity, a higher power etc.

Whatever name you give it doesn't change the outcome and I thank you all for taking this journey with me.

Most importantly I am grateful for having had the good fortune of being born in the United States. A country that gives me the freedom to write and share this book. A country that although not perfect, but whose foundation supports the freedom to think and speak freely.

My wish is that every person in the world to be given these basic human rights, the ones they were born with.

Then we will all be truly free...

Table of Contents

MALIBU

The constant rhythmic rocking of the train gave a false sense of comfort to the surreal circumstance I had found myself in. This would be the first day of a two-day trip crossing Turkey to the Iranian border. It was 1986.

The train cabin was old and showed signs of a very long, hard life, archaic really. Everything was covered with a thick brown dust, including me. I could taste it on my lips and no amount of wiping made it go away.

There was nothing but pitch-blackness outside the train window; no city lights in the distance or anything that could be seen reflecting life outside the train. Odd flickering lights inside the cabin were the only things that gave off any light. Sitting across from me were three young Middle Eastern men, their bodies squished against one another—clearly too large a mass for one bench seat, but they were too shy to sit next to a young American woman. So, I sat alone.

Just hours before we had all been strangers, and now, we were swapping life stories. I twisted my ring around my finger, trying to focus my thoughts on happier times, anywhere but here.

My thoughts took me back to 1977. I had just turned 21. I was a native Californian and attending a local college while deciding what I was going to be when I grew up, and truthfully growing up was not part of my curriculum. My daily goal was to hurry up and get through whatever the class of the day was so I could get down to the beach and surf.

I tucked a textbook under my arm, only for looks of course. The book was never opened. But I put forth a lot of effort trying not to damage it so I could sell it next semester at the used book sale for a better price. I don't think I ever sold a book that didn't have a little sand embedded in it somewhere. Maybe it would be a calling card to its next reader.

Looks were deceiving. I looked like the stereotype of a surfer—tan, blonde highlighted hair with strips of gold, and blue eyes that blended with the blues of the ocean—but I was a lousy surfer. I swam like a fish and had wide feet, which made me good at balancing on the board and looking the part. But it was nothing but a façade. My real love was taking my board out past the waves and bobbing about mindlessly.

With book and board, I arrived at Malibu Beach. Standing in front of my dark blue convertible Mustang, I surveyed the coast. It was another day in paradise. The sun was busy tanning all the bodies laid out beneath it on white sandy beaches that stretched as far as the eye could see. Tumbling in front of us was the blue Pacific Ocean with white caps, warning us of the possibility of drama beneath the waves. But none of that mattered. This was my backyard, my playground, the world I had been dropped into since birth, and I loved it. I loved it no matter what weather the wind brought to its shore. It was all beautiful to me.

I could see my girlfriends, Debbie and Susan, already lying out and swapping life's daily dramas. We never seemed to run out of those stories. They were not real to anyone but us and, at our age, we had a lot of them.

Debbie was a tall brunette who had always wanted to be a blonde. As soon as she laid out her towel on the beach, she was spritzing lemon juice and a product called Sun In through her hair, asking if I could see any highlights. I lied. It made her feel good, and it made me feel good seeing her beam when I said I could. The strong smell of baby oil and sand between my toes told me I had made it back to Nirvana.

"You should have seen the hot guy that just walked by, Lara!" Susan announced.

"I'm sorry I missed it."

"Liar!" Debbie threw a towel in my direction.

I dropped my book and towel and sat between my friends.

It was common knowledge that I avoided what I called "boys." At my age, they could be so incredibly stupid, egotistical, and with the introspection of a pollywog. I found myself always forgiving them for their downfalls, thinking that it must be part of the progression of growing into a human being. Don't get me wrong; I did love the male energy. As juvenile as they were, they piqued my interest as to what made them tick. But, at this point in my life, I didn't want one of my own. They were best looked to for entertainment purposes only. I watched as countless young women fell into deep depression over what they saw as the loss of the love of their lives, their other half, their Prince Charming. I didn't want any part of it. I didn't need a prince.

"It's rough out there, Lara. We're waiting it out," Susan announced.

Susan was a bit of a tomboy, a fantastic surfer, and a great friend. She could not care less about what anyone had to say about her because most of her thoughts had not landed in this world.

It was a job to keep up a conversation with Susan, but well worth the effort when she tied it all together in the end.

"What's that smell?" I asked.

The ocean carried with it an array of odors. Some were so amazing that it was a wonder no one had found a way to bottle them, although many had tried to capture Sea Breeze, Clear Water, etc. But this smell was not like any I had ever sensed before. My nose took me to Debbie's spot on her towel. I gave her the "spit it out" look.

"Fine, it's my new homemade sun lotion." Debbie held up a large spray bottle with a dark brown liquid in it.

Susan jumped in, "It's chamomile tea. I swear it's putting me to sleep, Lara!"

I took the bottle, spraying it in my hands. "It's not giving you a tan, Debbie; you're staining your skin!"

Long discolored streaks could be seen running down Debbie's legs.

Susan burst into laughter. Debbie grabbed the bottle, spraying it on her legs and trying to blend the mixture of colors.

The ocean waves caught my attention. I watched as they crashed onto the shore and noticed several young guys struggling with a surfboard. One would attempt to stand up on the board while the other two held it. Down they'd go, over and over again.

"Okay, this is sad. Maybe we should help them?" I shared.

"Hell no, this is hysterical. You're such a goody two shoes, Lara!" That was what it sounded like to be chastised by Debbie, but I didn't care.

"Yeah, Pollyanna!" Susan chimed in. I shot Susan a surprised look. "Sorry, Lara, but it's true," she added.

I stood up, standing firmly in the sand, holding my position with my friends. "You know, none of us was born knowing how to surf."

"I was four years old," Susan shared.

Actually, it probably was inbred with Susan. She had a way of instinctively owning a board more than anyone I knew. I looked at my snub friends, whom I dearly loved, but I knew that breaking away from the pack was needed at this moment.

I grabbed my board and tried to march away as dramatically as possible with a sand-covered butt, foolishly trying to make a point to my friends. They laughed.

"She's going to ruin it. Yep, there she goes!" Debbie kicked up sand in protest.

As I approached the three young men, I noticed they looked to be in their twenties with an "I'm an adult who can't focus" attitude. It was also apparent they were not local. They spoke another language with thick accents, but their laughter was universal.

"You guys need any help?" I asked.

They turned and looked in my direction. What had looked like three kids having fun quickly turned into three men attempting to be cool. The one trying to stand up on the board was boyishly handsome, tall with olive-colored skin, two matching dimples, one on each cheek, a split chin, and black curls that fell down his neck. He immediately jumped off the board. If he could have strutted in two feet of water, he would have.

"We're good," he answered proudly.

The shorter, cocky one attempted to assure me that in their country, this was how they surfed. I smiled at the three, who were looking for my approval.

"And what country would that be?" I asked.

"We're Persian, from Iran," said the one who stayed closest to the shore. He was slight in build and much more timid than the other two. My blank stare must have shown them that I had no idea where that was.

The tall one instinctively answered my question. "Where Persian rugs come from. We're foreign exchange students from the Middle East. I'm Kayan."

He said the words with pride in his voice and seemed to stand a little taller. A silly sight considering he was covered in sand with blobs of the mixture dripping off strands of hair in front of his face.

I held out my hand. "Lara." Kayan awkwardly shook my hand. "Okay, well, if you need any help… Careful, the waves are rough today." I turned to leave.

"No, don't go. We don't know what we're doing. My friends are going to kill me!" Kayan blurted, as if he couldn't get the words out fast enough. He finished it off with a boyish smile that was hard to look away from.

For a moment there was something—not a bad something, a comfortable something, as if we already knew and liked each other, not in a romantic way but as two people. I didn't spend much time analyzing my feelings. I really wanted to surf, but it was an odd feeling. Maybe it was the earnestness in Kayan's voice, or how he went from cool to sincere in half a second. I waved Debbie and Susan over. They pretended to look away, but then reluctantly joined us with their boards.

"This is Hamid and Farzad," Kayan added.

Hamid was the short one with the most attitude. I think he had some of that Napoleon thing going on. Farzad, on the other hand, was slight in build, and if I was to give him a label, it would be the intellectual one. He was busy sizing everything up: the waves, the size of the boards.

"I'm not sure the board can safely handle two people," Farzad mumbled.

"Really? Well, the only way we'll find out is if we try it. Trust me, the board can handle it," I answered and dropped my board into the water. Hamid, the cocky one, perked up as Debbie and Susan approached. I motioned for Kayan to get on the board behind me. He stood frozen.

"You're going to need more than two feet of water to surf, Mr. Middle East." He was scared. I didn't know if it was of surfing or me.

"Whatever you say, Miss California. Or is it Mrs.?"

A small wave jumped over the board, hitting us. Rather than moving with the wave, Kayan seemed to take a stand, challenging it. He tucked his arms under his shoulders like a small chick and started mumbling what sounded like Middle Eastern prayers.

"Can you and your friends swim, Kayan?" I nervously asked.

Kayan put his hand on the board, steadying himself in the water. "Of course we can swim. We don't have a Malibu like you do, or homes with swimming pools, but when we go on vacations, we have beaches and lakes."

"Okay then, get on." I patted the board.

I looked back at the others. Hamid struggled to be cool and stay on his feet at the same time.

He jumped on the back of Debbie's board and promptly fell off. Debbie was already annoyed with her partner.

"Maybe I should hold on to you?" Hamid suggested.

"If you plan on dying today," Debbie replied.

I knew I would have to pay a price for suggesting we help this group of out-of-towners. It wouldn't be my first price nor my last.

Out in the water, everyone separated. I was in my element. The sun was shining on the water's ripples, left behind by the waves. The calming sensation that came with it caused me to lose myself in the experience until I felt Kayan's shaking body against my back.

"Are you okay?" I asked.

"Yes," Kayan answered.

I turned back to look at my passenger, who was shaking with a mixture of cold and fear.

"Let's get in the water, you'll warm up." I jumped off the board.

Kayan shook his head no. I swam around the board, trying to show him it was safe, but he only shook his head harder.

"Okay, you'll probably freeze." I started to swim away.

"No, don't go, come back!"

In a panic, Kayan threw himself off the board and under the water he went. I swam back to him, but he was gone. In high school I had been certified as a life-guard. It was either that or folk dancing. I searched my mind for the memory of how to save a swimmer, pre-paring to save a life, but now it was all a big blur. Mr. Middle East was going to die, and it was all my fault!

"Hey, you're right. It is much warmer." I turned to see Kayan swimming behind me with his big smile, bob-bing in and out of the water. I splashed at his face.

"Okay, okay!" Kayan splashed me back and the game was on. Like two kids, we chased each other, en-joying the warmer than normal water, finally resting our tired bodies against the board.

"You win," Kayan announced, as if there had even been a close moment in our battle. Not his fault, ob-viously. His swimming experience was limited. "In my country men and women are not allowed to go to the beach together. Some beaches have long curtains sepa-rating men and women in the water," he shared.

I could see his thoughts remembering the experience. "Why?" I asked, trying to grasp what he had just said.

"It's a Muslim country, and women are supposed to be covered up and protected from men looking at them."

"Get out!" I replied.

"Okay." Kayan started to pull himself up on the board. I pulled him back into the water. "No, I didn't mean to get out of the water. It's a saying, like something is unbelievable."

Kayan looked at me, about as puzzled as anyone could be, and I looked at him in the same way, trying to comprehend who this stranger was.

That night we had a bonfire on the beach. Like moths, people were drawn to it. It didn't take much to make a party at the beach. Kayan and his friends fit right in. They started their own soccer competition between the surfers and themselves. They were great players. The locals didn't have a chance. A lot of sand was eaten that day, and it wasn't by our new friends.

The ball bounced off heads, elbows, and knees. It was as if the ball was an extension of their bodies. They relished in taking advantage of the inexperienced locals. Hamid now had surfing stories to tell all the girls, and the waves grew bigger each time he told one.

"Hey, there you are!" I turned to see Kayan standing behind me, dropping a soccer ball at his feet.

"Yep, here I am. I saw you guys playing; very impressive," I added.

Kayan's already larger-than-life smile beamed.

"You surf, we play football. That's what we call it. Here you call it soccer, but this is our football; very important in my country."

"You must miss your country?" I was curious to hear why someone would leave their life as they knew it and travel across the world.

Kayan paused, took off his shirt, and wrapped it around my shoulders. It was the first time anyone had done that, and it felt good, protective, and intimate. I allowed myself a moment to enjoy the feelings before I started questioning what was really behind the shirt covering my shoulders and thinking about handing it back—which I didn't.

We both sat down in the now cold sand. "Yes, I have a big family. I have seven brothers and sisters. I'm the oldest boy."

I interrupted. "Seven brothers and sisters?"

"And my parents, that makes ten of us. What about you? Any brothers or sisters?"

"I have one older brother and of course my parents, but they're divorced."

"Ah, we don't have much divorce. In the Middle East you're stuck with whom you marry."

We both laughed. A guy with a sense of humor. Rare. Most were so busy trying to build themselves up, it was sometimes difficult to find out who they really were.

"Will you go back to your country when you finish school?" I asked.

"That is my plan. Once I get my engineering degree, I will go home. But there are things about my country I don't miss." Kayan's tone changed. "My country is not like here. In my country we have a dictatorship. We cannot speak freely or share what we think. You could be killed or put in prison for that. I will miss the freedom I have here."

Kayan drew circles in the sand, one representing Iran and one representing the United States, and a monster with seaweed hair next to Iran. I listened intently while this stranger described to me a piece of his world that I had no idea existed and, more importantly, what it all meant to him. Kayan explained how a dictator, called the Shah, ruled Iran with a very heavy hand. In order to keep the citizens of Iran under his control, the Shah allowed very little communication with the outside world. Having a phone was a luxury experienced by few. News was given, not reported, and the Shah was supported by his Secret Service called the Savak. Even the name sounded ominous. Kayan also shared stories of people disappearing after being dragged out of their homes in the middle of the night by the Savak. Rumors were spread about the person having said something against the government or a neighbor turning them in as a traitor. The stories were terrifying to me, but Kayan told them like he was talking about any local neighborhood. He smashed his hand into the monster he had made in the sand.

"Is that why you came to the United States?" I asked.

"I came to the United States to go to school. Schools here are much better than those in Iran. You go to school, too. I saw your book. I like a smart woman."

Inside I was having a hard time not laughing, knowing I was barely skating by in any class. I was hardly a scholar. "Yes, education is very important." I smirked and turned my head, hoping he didn't see it.

When I turned back, Kayan brushed his hand over my cheek. "Sand," he said.

I brushed at my face, laughing. "I wonder where that came from?"

Kayan leaned in and kissed me. I'd like to say I wasn't expecting it, but inside I was thinking, *Middle Eastern boys are slow*. It wasn't one of those lustful kisses like I'd had with other guys; there was gentleness about it. I kissed him back, breaking all my own self-imposed rules.

"I'd better go," I mumbled through the kiss, hoping he'd stop me.

"Okay," he mumbled back, but we continued to kiss.

I reached to hand him his shirt, but he put his hand over mine, stopping me. "No, give it back to me the next time we see each other."

Normally a presumptuous line like that would have gotten him his shirt back immediately, but I wanted to see him again. There was no logic to my reaction other than that I liked him.

"Dinner tomorrow night? No, lunch? What about breakfast?" Kayan rambled.

I didn't know how to respond. Kayan looked into my eyes. "That is my favorite shirt, you know. I like you, Lara. I've given you something very valuable to me. What is your last name, in case I need to find you?"

"Anderson. What's yours?" I asked.

Kayan smiled. "Oh, you're going to be impressed. Are you ready?"

I nodded yes.

"Batmanglij."

I laughed. "Really?"

Kayan nodded. "Yep. Impressive, yes? Come on, say it."

I laughed and stumbled through saying his name. "Like Batman!"

My analogy had been lost on Kayan. He had no idea what I was talking about. We were two people who up until now had lived in two different worlds.

Someone on the beach was playing loud music— "Never Gonna Give You Up" sung by Barry White. The singer's deep voice had a way of vibrating through a person's soul. Kayan jumped to his feet and pulled me to him. He moved passionately to the music. It was obvious dancing was not a talent he possessed, but we both danced as if we were in a competition anyway. He swung me around, dipped me at all the wrong times, made funny faces just to see me laugh—and I did. When the song stopped, Kayan leaned down and covered me with his long arms. I could feel him sigh while holding me. I felt myself relax in this stranger's hold, and then he kissed me, not once but twice. His height put me at a disadvantage. My feet could barely touch the sand.

"Wait." Kayan picked me up and carried me to a sandy knoll, slowly lowering me until we were at the same height. He mumbled through another kiss, "Now we have our own song!"

I laughed, not thinking much about it. That night when I got home, my phone rang. It was Kayan. We talked for hours, mostly laughing, mostly at ourselves!

II

MR. MIDDLE EAST

When I asked Kayan why he chose California, his answer was simple. "They gave me a visa."

Visas weren't easy to get, but Kayan had set his intention on going to college in the United States. When California said yes, it was nothing more than the luck of the draw.

From that point on, Kayan and I became inseparable. All the silly clichés fit; neither of us could think of a day without the other. It wasn't a crippling kind of relationship. It was pure and simple; it just was.

I would have liked to be able to say I moved cautiously in the relationship, using my left brain as well as my right, but caution never entered the room. I had just met my best friend, and we had a lifetime to catch up on.

One day Kayan showed up at the apartment I shared with Carol and Richard, my two roommates from college. Richard opened the door and was immediately given the stink eye from Kayan. No matter how often they saw each other, Kayan could not accept my having a male roommate, but he'd have to get over it. I wasn't giving in to such silliness.

"Lara, that guy is here," Richard announced. Richard wasn't making the situation any better.

I rushed to the door and jumped into Kayan's arms. "You mean my guy?" Kayan spun me around.

"Whatever," Richard mumbled as he left the room.

"I have a surprise, Lara." Kayan pulled out two tickets. I watched him bend down as he retrieved a metal pie tin off the porch step that had bright green grass growing in it.

I bypassed the grass and grabbed the tickets, reading them out loud. "Celebrate Nowruz at UCLA College, dinner included." I stumbled over the words, looking at Kayan for an explanation since neither of us went to UCLA.

"Nowruz is the Persian New Year. It's our biggest holiday!"

With great excitement in his voice, Kayan went on to explain Nowruz. He explained that it wasn't a religious holiday, like most; it was a celebration that always begins at the spring equinox, usually in March when the sun crosses the equator, and day and night are of equal lengths. He moved the plate of grass in front of me.

"We celebrate all things new. We clean our homes and our closets to make room for new things to come, like you coming into my life. I want to celebrate Nowruz with you, Lara." Kayan bent over and kissed me.

"Nice grass. Most guys bring flowers," Richard said as he walked through the room.

The night of the Nowruz celebration, Kayan was like a child at Christmas. Whatever this holiday was, it was special to him. So, dressed in our finery, we entered the huge hall that had been set up for Nowruz on the highly respected campus of UCLA. I was shocked to see hundreds of people from the Middle East, young and old, all inside socializing in the beautifully decorated hall. They, too, were excited to be there, which piqued my interest in the holiday even more.

Kayan proudly took my hand, escorting me around the hall. There were displays with beautiful colored and decorated eggs, spring flowers, more plates of green grass and several bowls with goldfish swimming in them.

Kayan pointed to the table. "The table is called a Haftseen. Like the grass, everything here means something; the eggs are for birth."

"What do the goldfish mean?" I asked.

"Life, they represent life, and after the two weeks of Nowruz, we release them."

"Where, where do you release them?"

Kayan gave me a blank look. "I don't know, maybe a nice lake somewhere."

"Well, I hope it's not someone's toilet."

Kayan stared at me. "I'm sure they go to a nice place. I remember my father being in charge of taking care of the goldfish."

I looked at Kayan as if to say, *Are you sure they weren't flushed?*

Kayan took my hand and led me away to a huge oval table with tray upon tray of food, which consisted of colorful rice dishes, a green baked vegetable dish that had been cut into squares, and plates of some kind of white fish. The best part was a table covered in an array of endless sweets. Kayan saw my eyes gloss over admiring the desserts.

"Come on." He handed me a plate and started filling it up.

I couldn't help but notice I was one of maybe a handful of guests who by appearance were not Persian. I was a minority for the first time in my life. I don't think I would have been uncomfortable if it weren't for the obvious look of discomfort on the faces of the other Persian guests due to my presence. Everyone was speaking Farsi, making conversations limited. But Kayan never took his attention away from me, which made me feel all the more special. He found a table that was a bit more secluded for us to sit at, which suited us perfectly. It was as if no one else was in the room.

"In Iran we have fireworks, all over the city of Tehran. The skies light up!"

As we ate, Kayan shared stories of celebrating Nowruz as a child. He talked about having hard-boiled egg wars, where you would bang your egg against an opponent's egg, and the one with the least amount of damage was the winner.

That night I felt like I had officially entered Kayan's world. Like two kids ditching a family event, we snuck out early and wound up at Kayan's apartment, which he shared with Hamid and Farzad. We passionately kissed our way up the stairs.

"Wait, wait right here. Don't go anywhere!" Kayan nervously fidgeted with the lock and ducked inside the apartment. I could hear loud whispers and doors banging and saw the lights suddenly go out. His long arm reached from behind the door and pulled me into his apartment. There was a heavy smell of air freshener, tropical I thought. I was glad Kayan had turned out the lights. The last time I'd seen the apartment it had screamed *bachelors live here*...definitely not romantic.

Kayan picked me up and carried me into his bedroom while kicking his way through the clothes, soccer balls, and miscellaneous empty food packages, only putting me down when there was an empty space big enough to do so. Like Houdini, in one flick of a blanket, he cleared the bed. I broke out laughing. He tried his best to keep the mood, kissing me before tripping over a pair of sneakers and landing on top of me. We broke out into belly laughs, and Kayan rolled onto his back.

"This wasn't exactly the way I had envisioned our night together. I'm sorry. I wanted everything to be special for you, Lara."

"You are special," I whispered. I looked him in the eyes, rubbing my fingers over the details of his face, and kissed him passionately. "Happy Nowruz," I whispered through the kiss.

There was nothing outside ourselves that could have made our first night together any more special than it was. I felt like a wall had been taken down inside me and replaced by a feeling of oneness with another. Kayan had touched a part of me I didn't know existed, and it was a feeling I never wanted to end. After our love-making, we silently lay in the bed. Kayan pulled at a corner of the blanket to cover me.

"You are always protecting me from the cold. This is California," I said.

Kayan kissed my naked shoulders. "I love you, Lara Anderson. I loved you from the first time we met standing in the ocean when you came to save me."

Hundreds of thoughts entered my mind and swirled in my head. Was that the unusual, odd feeling I had the day we met? It felt good hearing someone tell me they loved me. No, it felt good hearing Kayan say he loved me. I took a deep breath, stopping the words from exiting my mouth, thinking about what the words "I love you" would do to the seemingly perfect life we had together. After all, we had only known each other for three months. Didn't love need more time to grow than that? I quickly decided I should hold them inside where they would be safe—and then, without a conscious thought, the words betrayed me and flew from my mouth.

"I love you, too, Kayan Batmanglij."

Kayan immediately grabbed me in his arms. I had said it, I had meant it, and there was no taking it back; I didn't want to. For the first time in my life, I was in love…

Six months later, we took a big step and moved in together. If we weren't physically together, we were on the phone talking as if we were. It seemed to be the normal progression.

I found a cute little apartment with a manmade lake. I called it a pretend lake that even came with a few token ducks. "Pretend ducks," Kayan called them. We loved our pretend world. But there were definitely differences in who we were, like on the day we moved in.

"Are we done yet?" Kayan fell back onto the couch, surrounded by the bits and pieces of two people's lives.

"Kayan Batmanglij!" I admonished.

Kayan slowly rolled his head in my direction. "I love when you say my name."

"That's because no one else can!" I threw myself on top of him. Kissing him almost made me forget the chaos around us. "We really need to finish bringing in the boxes," I mumbled under the kiss.

"Are you happy, Lara?"

"I'm very happy, Kayan, but we really need to unpack these boxes."

I had taken a job with the City of Los Angeles helping families with children who were in some sort of distress. I loved my job, and showing up on Monday meant I'd have to be able to get to my wardrobe.

"I wanted to talk to you about that, Lara. We have far too much stuff. I came to this country with one bag, across thousands of miles. One bag." Kayan picked up a large green duffle bag and let it drop to the ground, giving himself a dramatic visual.

"I was going to ask you about that. What's this?" I pulled out of my pocket a bracelet of golden beads and held it up to Kayan.

"My tasbih. You found it!" He snatched the beads from my hand, kissing them like a long-lost friend.

"What is it?" I asked, watching him roll the beads from finger to finger.

"Here they call them prayer or worry beads, but in my country, it's called a tasbih. They are what got me here. I prayed over and over again to come to the United States to go to college, where I would fall in love with the most beautiful woman. See? They work."

I grabbed the beads and started rubbing them in my hand. "You said you weren't religious. Is this a Muslim tradition?" I asked.

Kayan took my fingers and slowly moved them over the beads. "Not religious. They belonged to my grandfather and my great-grandfather before that. They were handed down to me because I am the oldest son."

I rubbed the beads in my hands; they felt cool and smooth as glass. "Make my boyfriend the strongest, fastest mover in the world!" I said.

Kayan grabbed the beads and stood up. "They don't always work!"

I handed him the closest box. Afraid I'd lose his attention from the task at hand, I pointed to the word "bedroom" written boldly in big black letters on the side. We both looked at the box in his hands filled with stuffed animals.

Kayan pulled out a stuffed dog. "Why?"

I grabbed the dog. "I can't believe you said that to Snoozy!"

He took the dog back and looked it in the face. "Why?"

We did have differences, some of which we accepted we'd never connect on, but most of which I felt a delight in. The leftover ones were what self-help books were written for. Kayan sighed and slowly started to walk away with the box. "What if I don't want to live with animals watching me sleep or make love?"

I kissed Kayan and handed him the prayer beads. "Try these."

A duck's loud quacking got our attention. There, in the middle of our new living room, stood an angry and very hungry duck that proceeded to approach us.

"Kayan, do something!" I screamed.

Kayan chased after the duck, herding it towards the door. "The bum sleeping in front of my old apartment door looks pretty good right now, doesn't he?"

It turned out everyone loved Kayan; my family and friends found him as endearing as I did, even my racist father. His being from Iran was nothing more than a novelty to those who met him. At the time, Iran was not on anyone's radar. It was an oil-rich country halfway around the world that no one knew much about, but our government did. We were deeply dependent on oil. My father, who followed politics, was careful not to say anything involving race in my presence. He knew a battle would follow from his colorblind daughter, having made that mistake many times before. But when it came to Kayan, he didn't have an unkind word.

I remember one Christmas Eve when my family gathered at our new home to celebrate, Kayan and my father bonded over some electronic gadget that Kayan had dismantled.

"That's quite clever, young man." My father was fixated on the gadget. Kayan proudly handed it to my father.

"Did you learn electronics in Iran?" My father assumed Kayan's skills had to have something to do with his culture.

Kayan stopped and thought. "No, I just like figuring things out," he said, ruining my father's theory that everything about us was based on our race or sex.

"Can we figure out dinner? I'm starved," my brother Mark complained.

Mark was 25 years old, a bit overconfident with a hippie freak personality, emphasis on freak. He always wore bell-bottoms and a t-shirt that had a commentary written on the front of it. He had somewhat evolved and learned to clean up his clothing remarks around family. Within two minutes of talking to Mark, most people would find themselves shaking their heads and walking away. I think that had something to do with my feelings about men. I always shook my head and walked away.

"Don't be rude, Mark."

Chastising my brother was one of the duties my mother had taken on. She was the only one willing to waste her breath. My mom was a wise woman. She had divorced my father years ago but had the rare ability to still share space with her ex, especially with my father, who was a huge chauvinist and the king of telling you where a woman's place was. One year he bought me a typewriter for Christmas. His thinking was that all women should learn to cook and type to fulfill their place in society.

I, on the other hand, spent hours in my closet as a child pretending to be a DJ. With my new reel-to-reel tape recorder, I was going to go into the music field. It was my secret. I guess you could say I was a closet music entrepreneur. It also became quite clear at an early age that I couldn't type at all!

Kayan stood up. "Your brother is hungry."

"See, somebody that listens to me. You're a smart guy, K," Mark praised Kayan.

Kayan liked the approval, but I couldn't have him giving my brother that important a role. "We don't listen to Mark," I said.

Kayan looked at me like I was the cruelest person alive. He was about to get a lesson in American family dynamics.

"Dinner is ready," my mother announced.

My father had taken a seat at the head of the table. Mark immediately grabbed the seat at the other end.

My mother cleared her throat. "Not today, Mark. This is Kayan's home. He sits at the head of the table."

"No, no, that's okay. As long as I sit next to your daughter, I'm a happy man." Kayan put his arm around me.

My mom was obviously touched by Kayan's words, and in one swift move she smacked Mark on the side of his head.

Mark immediately rose and in a low voice spoke to Kayan. "That's so not cool, man."

My mom motioned for Kayan to sit at the head of the table, which he quickly did after seeing the repercussions of not doing what my mom said. I wondered how it had come about that it was a man's place to sit at the head of the table. I mean, who decided that? Obviously a man.

After dinner we decorated the Christmas tree. We were one of those families that decorated our tree and opened our gifts on Christmas Eve—a Scandinavian tradition, my father would say. Later I would find out it was my father's way of sleeping in on Christmas morning and had nothing to do with tradition.

Kayan heard a lot of "No, not like that" as he tried to be a part of the festivities. There were rules to holiday decorations, and my mom and I were pros. Kayan made the mistake of trying to correct us on the correctness of our holiday. "Jesus never had a tree," he proudly shared after he had done some research on Christianity. Everyone stopped and looked at him. He looked at me. I held back a smile and shook my head no.

My mom handed Kayan a tiny manger scene painted on a large silver glass ball and said, pointing to a tree in the picture, "You can put it right there, dear." Mom took his hand and guided it to the perfect spot.

I don't think I ever heard Kayan share insights on any of our holiday traditions again. The melting pot of America had many different ways of celebrating the same holiday. He quickly adjusted his thinking to accept it all.

I wanted to make a point of acknowledging Kayan's family in our lives, but it was hard to do with them being so far away and the lack of communication, so I framed pictures of his family and set them out to surprise him.

"Don't come in, Kayan!" Those were the wrong words to use with Kayan. It only made him move faster, which was exactly what he did, now standing over my shoulder.

"What's this?" Kayan picked up one of the pictures. I grabbed it back from him.

"You're messing up my order," I complained.

He began picking up the pictures and rearranging them and said, "Well, you've got it all wrong." He held up one of the pictures. "These three are my oldest sisters. They should be first."

I threw up my hands and watched while he went into detail on each family member and who they were to him. He had three older sisters, all married with children. Kayan was the oldest of four boys, and when he looked at his brothers' pictures, it was obvious he connected with them the most. He was their big brother, and I would later learn why birth order had a lot to do with a child's future in Iran. For a living, Kayan's father sold Persian rugs, and his mother was a housewife like the majority of Persian women at the time.

After rearranging the pictures, Kayan paused, admiring them. I handed him one last picture of his eight-year-old sister.

"Tala, the baby." Kayan placed the picture at the end of the rest.

"Happy now?" I quipped.

He turned towards me. "Thank you."

Kayan and I spent a lot of time appreciating having found one another. It wasn't like he was the boy next door, or I was the arranged marriage his parents were hoping for. The odds of the two of us meeting and then falling in love were practically nonexistent, and we recognized the gift we had been given.

III

THE PROMISE

One day Kayan insisted that he wanted to go surfing with me, which was surprising since he had made it obvious that surfing was not his thing. Even the ride through the canyon to get there made him nauseous.

"I told you that you didn't have to come with me," I said while watching Kayan pacing and taking deep breaths in the beach parking lot, fighting back the motion sickness.

"No, I know how much you love to surf. That's how we met, remember?"

He struggled to pull my board from the back seat of the Mustang. It was obvious he was not comfortable handling a board even if it was on land. I grabbed the front of the board while Kayan followed holding the back end.

"Of course I remember. It was only two years ago!" I answered.

"Well, I miss surfing."

I laughed to myself, knowing that wasn't true. Kayan was not comfortable surfing. To him, every wave represented the possibility of death. If the waves didn't kill him, it was sharks that he knew were circling. Quite honestly, I enjoyed the solitude of surfing; I didn't need a buddy.

We dropped the board in the water. It was an absolutely gorgeous day at the beach. Some would call it picture perfect: sunny, blue skies, and an ocean that had chosen to be several colors of blue and turquoise that day. A small group of fellow surfers passed carrying their boards.

"Hey, Lara, the waves are really rad today," one of them called out.

"Thanks," I answered.

"Maybe it's not good to surf today." Kayan's tone had shifted to one of nervousness.

I looked at him quizzically. "Why do you say that?' I asked.

"He said the waves are bad."

"What? Oh, he said they are rad; that means really good," I giggled.

"Does he mean good like they are big?" Kayan scanned the ocean.

"He means it's a good day to surf. Come on, get on." I patted the back of the board just like I had when we first met and, just like before, Kayan nervously got on. In fact, I don't think he had ever gone surfing with me again after our first meeting. Feeling his shaking body behind me as I paddled out brought back the fond memory of when we had first met.

"We don't have to go that far," he shared.

I turned and looked back at him. He was shaking just like before, and it wasn't from the cold. "You're the one that wanted to go surfing. What's going on?"

"Nothing. I know how you love to surf."

"Yes, but you don't have to go with me. I don't always go with you when you play soccer."

"But I love when you do, even if you cheer for me at the wrong times," Kayan laughed.

"You love my hot chocolate," I added.

"With those white balls in it!"

"Marshmallows," I responded.

"What?"

"They are called marshmallows. We can go back in if you want, Kayan."

"No, no, this is good. I like just sitting here."

"Okay, I'm going to go swim."

"No, no, stay here with me," he said in a panicked kind of tone.

I turned back and looked at him. "I'll be right back," I answered.

"You can be a very difficult woman, Lara!" Kayan said, fumbling with something in his hand.

"What's going on with you?" I asked.

Kayan was frustrated, which was not like him at all. I wondered if being in the ocean was causing him to have a panic attack. He suddenly stopped fidgeting and looked directly at me.

"I love you, Lara Anderson," he said affirmatively.

"I love you too," I answered.

"No, no, you're not listening to me! Let me say this. I loved you from the first day we met. I love the way you laugh; it's usually at me, but that's okay. I love the way you care for me and put those white balls in my hot chocolate. I want us to be always."

Although I appreciated the beautiful things Kayan was saying, I was getting concerned about his odd behavior.

"I love you, too, Kayan, but I think we should go back."

"No, we can't go back!" he shouted.

I was stunned. Kayan never raised his voice. "What's wrong with you?" I asked.

"I'm doing this all wrong. I wanted this to be perfect, and I know you love it out here more than anywhere."

He held out his hand, almost losing his balance. "Will you marry me, Lara Anderson? Will you share your life with me?"

Inside Kayan's hand was a beautiful ring with a diamond in the middle of a heart. I stared at the sight of Kayan in front of me, wibble-wobbling on the surfboard, holding out a ring with his larger-than-life smile. He had chosen my favorite place in life, the same beach on which we had met. He had braved the canyons, the fear of sharks, and the ocean to ask me to marry him.

"You're supposed to say yes."

Kayan was shaking so hard he almost shook himself off the board. I turned myself around to face him; the shaking wasn't from being cold, or the threat of sharks. No, it was much greater than that. It was from the fear of asking me to marry him. I saw his hand with the ring start to sway.

"Yes, I'll marry you!"

I quickly grabbed his hand with the ring, saving it from being dropped overboard, and excitedly kissed him, throwing us both into the water. Kayan grabbed the ring from me and slipped it onto my finger. We spent the rest of the day playing in the ocean just like we had done when we first met.

In 1983, two years after we met, Kayan and I married on a beach in California under an arch that my father made for us.

Everyone who mattered to us was there except Kayan's mother. She was the one person he wanted at our wedding. The distance and all the red tape were too much to make it happen. Plus, she had four more kids still at home to worry about. But on the day we got married, nothing really mattered. It did not matter that my flowers almost didn't make it, or that I decided I didn't like my dress.

Standing there looking out over the ocean and feeling Kayan put his calming hand into mine was all that mattered. That day we promised to love, honor, respect, and share our lives with one another, becoming Mr. and Mrs. Batmanglij.

IV

THE COUP

One day about a year after we were married, Kayan raced into our home and turned on the television, something he never did. I followed him over to where he stood, a foot away from the screen.

"What's going on?" I innocently asked.

The television screen showed people fighting and demonstrating in the streets of Tehran. People were chanting "Death to America!" while standing in front of the American Embassy. A life-sized dummy dressed as Uncle Sam swung from a fence and was set on fire. I had never seen Kayan so distraught.

"There's been a coup in Iran, and they took over the American Embassy!"

I dropped to the floor next to Kayan. There was no way I could grasp what was going on or his reaction to it. I had to think about what the word "coup" meant; everyone on the news was saying the word over and over again. And then the meaning came back to me. A coup was when one government was overthrown, most likely illegally, by another. As it turned out, it was primarily the young people of Iran who started the coup by protesting the Shah and his government. They wanted change, they wanted freedom! It was a dangerous move to disagree with a dictator, but they passionately demonstrated in the streets of Tehran. The Shah and his army responded violently to the uprise, creating battles within the city. Many, mostly the young, lost their lives. The fuse had been lit.

We would later learn the dissension in Iran was not just about hate and overthrowing the Shah; a few years prior, the Shah had felt threatened by the growing popularity amongst young students of a religious leader named Ayatollah Khomeini. In response, the Shah had Khomeini exiled from the country, thinking he had solved the problem. But it was Khomeini who was partially behind the coup, and the Shah was forced to flee Iran, leaving Khomeini to rule the country. Even the Shah's own army turned on him. One dictator had been traded for another; however, Khomeini raised the stakes by lacing everything he did with the label of Allah (God).

Retaliation was in the air for the rebels and, after years of repression, someone had to pay. The list was long. Taking the American Embassy was just a start, one that got the world's attention.

The new regime supported the takeover in retaliation for the United States giving sanction to the fleeing Shah.

Up until that time, embassies were known to be safehouses. The headquarters for a country's government to serve in a foreign country, an embassy was highly respected by the host government. But not only had the American Embassy been taken by Iranian rebels, more importantly, they took 52 American Embassy workers hostage. The streets in front of the embassy were packed with locals chanting and holding up banners that read "Down with the United States" and just about any other country you could think of. There were also signs denouncing the Shah and his government. The fact that it was the young people who started the unrest intensified Kayan's fear for his younger brothers.

"I have to talk to my family; I have to make sure they are okay," Kayan said in a daze.

I watched like a voyeur as Kayan tried to get a phone call out to his one neighbor who miraculously had a phone. There were loud electronic screeches, recordings of foreign voices that cut in and out, and Kayan's disappointed reaction each time he was disconnected.

Hamid and Ali showed up at the door. They greeted Kayan and me as if someone had died, and, in many ways, that was true. The country they knew and loved was gone, for better or worse. It would never be the same.

An array of emotions flew about the room: confusion, loss, mourning, anger, it was all there. No one owned one emotion more than another. Speaking in Persian, the three spoke quickly, sharing their insights and opinions on what was happening in Iran. At one point, Kayan stopped talking and looked at me. "I'm sorry, Lara, we don't mean to leave you out." He kissed me on top of my head.

"I understand," I said, which I didn't. "I'll make everyone something to eat."

As I entered the kitchen, their voices lowered and quickly filled with anger. I was glad I was no longer in the room. I tried to understand what was being said. There was obvious dissension amongst them, and they now resembled a football huddle, not wanting the other team to hear what they had to say. Was I the other team or was it anyone who wasn't them?

Our lives revolved around the news after that day. There was still no word from his family and no way to reach them. Kayan was glued to every report, looking for something that would give him peace and stop the fear he felt, especially for his brothers. However, nothing we watched on television gave anyone peace. At one point, the United States sent several military helicopters in to retrieve the hostages, called "Operation Eagle Claw." Unfortunately, there was a collision between the helicopters and six American soldiers were killed. Jimmy Carter was president at the time and took full responsibility. No matter how you looked at it, it was a tragedy.

"Hamid said Khomeini put a hit out on Carter. Crazy, huh?" Kayan said, never looking away from the television.

I didn't know how to respond. I didn't know how to respond to most of what was going on. I would calmly listen to Kayan when he shared the stories, being as supportive as possible. Even Kayan had not chosen a side.

"What about you, Kayan? Do you hate the United States?"

Kayan stopped watching the television and looked at me. "Me? No. You know I don't hate anything. I love it here. I understand the feeling. My country has been ruled by a dictator a long time, and most Persians believe the United States helped put the Shah in power."

"Is that what you believe?" I asked.

Kayan shook his head no. "I don't know. It's probably true, but this Khomeini guy, I don't trust him either. I just want my family to be okay."

I scooted next to him and rested my head on his shoulder while he continued to watch the breaking stories. The hostage situation had understandably enraged most Americans; they may not have known who the Iranians were before, but they now spewed the same hatred they saw on the television back at Iran. Everyone wanted everyone dead. They all had their own reasons why, but the outcome was the same.

During those months while we waited to hear about the well-being of Kayan's family, the peace we had once felt seemed to have dramatically left. Every night we, with the rest of the country, would watch a new television show that had been created for the hostage crisis called "Nightline." It was hosted by Ted Koppel. Every night the show would update America with what they knew about the hostages and the takeover. American citizens were frustrated. Why would a country they didn't even know want to take revenge on them? It was beyond their understanding.

Hostilities continued to grow, not just against Iran, but against anyone who was from Iran or looked Middle Eastern. People were hypersensitive as they worked out their feelings against this new threat, and they weren't hiding how they felt!

One day as we were crossing the parking lot at the supermarket and laughing over some silly thing, we passed a car with a bumper sticker that featured Mickey Mouse giving the finger with the words "Fuck Iran." Our laughter stopped.

"Don't pay attention, Kayan. Just stupid people."

Kayan put his arm around my neck. "My protector, it's okay. I hear it everywhere. School, work."

I stopped and looked at him. "You never said anything."

He casually responded, "What's to say? People are angry, I get it."

Anyone from Iran became an open target for abuse. It was really Kayan's and my first experience with racism. Although we felt safe in our own little world, it became obvious that Kayan represented an entire country that others hated.

Shortly before the hostage situation, Kayan had taken a job with an engineering company, his chosen profession. It was a low-level position, but he had hopes of future opportunities. Several of his co-workers expressed that they didn't hold his being from Iran against him. He knew it was their way of giving him their approval, but Kayan didn't know he needed anyone's approval. When did his being from Iran change who he was, who he had been for the last six months? Our lives were changing more than we could ever know.

One afternoon the phone rang, and as I picked it up, I immediately recognized the screeching sounds.

"Kayan!" I screamed and ran through the house looking for him. He was trapped behind the dryer, trying to fix an annoying sound.

"What is it, Lara? Are you okay?" Kayan struggled to remove himself from behind the machine.

I excitedly held out the phone. "I think it's Iran!"

He hurdled over the dryer and took the phone. While I was celebrating in the kitchen, the call quickly went from excitement to a sorrow like I had never witnessed before.

Kayan started yelling into the phone, "No, Ma, Ma, no!"

Not much else was said that I understood. A blank look and a flood of tears overtook Kayan's face. Still holding the phone, he dropped to his knees with a grieving wail.

It was one of those moments that, as much as you try to erase it, will never really go away. I held him, not knowing what had occurred.

Little by little the story unveiled itself. The long awaited and anticipated call wasn't the joyous one we had both hoped for. "My brother Ali was killed fighting against the Shah during the coup," Kayan sobbed against my shoulder.

"I'm so sorry, Kayan."

I knew nothing of death, nothing about war. I didn't even know what to do with the words. After all, what do you do when someone dies, especially a young man fighting in a war?

What could I say to my husband, my best friend, to make any of it better?

So, I didn't say a word. I sat there listening to everything that came out of him, even when it was in another language. Kayan's mother had told him it had taken her weeks to find Ali's body. Hundreds of bodies lay waiting in airplane hangars to be identified by loved ones. The imagery alone was horrific.

Kayan was devastated. His family was devastated. Then, he looked me in the eyes and said, "Lara, my mom asked me to come home to visit."

A debilitating fear unleashed inside of me as if it had been a Trojan horse waiting for this moment.

"Don't worry, Lara."

Did Kayan say those words?

I jumped to my feet. "Don't worry? They are still fighting, Kayan; your brother was just killed. Rebels have taken hostages. For God's sake, please think about what you are saying!"

My rant and list of all the reasons why this was a horrible decision continued for some time. Why would Kayan's mother want to put her son in such jeopardy?

I felt Kayan's fingers tapping on my back like you would do to console a baby. His outlook on the situation was very different from my own. He looked at Iran as the home he grew up in. He didn't see the war or political climate as a threat. To him, he was invincible.

My frustration was stifling. I wanted to shake him, to bring him to his senses, but nothing I said changed anything.

"I need to grieve with my family. I need to know they are okay," Kayan repeated over and over again.

And what if they're not okay? I thought. *Then what?*

I quickly chased those thoughts away and made the decision to try to see the situation through his eyes. He would go back for a visit, have the time he needed with his family, and come home—our home. Saying those words to myself didn't change the feelings I had about him going back to Iran. I was terrified, but no amount of my kicking and screaming would change anything. He was set on going.

Fortunately, there was lots of red tape before Kayan would be able to travel to Iran, and each step of the way

I prayed he would be unsuccessful, making it impossible for him to go. First, he had to get a visa from the Iranian Consulate in Washington. Surely with all that was happening in Iran, they would not approve such a thing. When the letter came, which I knew would upset him, I prepared myself to be the consoler and make it all better. I handed him the envelope confidently, watching while he opened it and removed a letter and his passport. I tried not to show my glee while he read it.

"They gave me my visa," Kayan said and handed me the letter, pointing to the bold black ink emblem imprinted inside his passport.

Kayan tried to downplay his excitement in front of me. I carefully looked at the passport, knowing there had to be a mistake. The writing was in Persian, so if there was one, I would have no idea. I felt like the wind had been knocked out of me, the blood rushing from my face. I started to cry. I wanted to tear it up, maybe mistakenly drop it down the garbage disposal and chop it up into a million little pieces.

It was Kayan who became the consoler. He held me tightly, whispering in my ear, "It's going to be okay; I promise. I'll be back before you know it."

Kayan had gotten everything he had asked for. His teachers and bosses at work approved his request to take a leave due to losing a family member. He had gotten everything except for my blessing, and I just didn't have it in me.

But like a Stepford wife, I gave him a farewell dinner, and, like a Stepford wife, I played my loving and supportive role. Hamid and Farzad came with notes and envelopes of money that Kayan was to give to their families in Tehran. Debbie and Susan came to be my support and glared at Kayan for being a horrible husband; girls are good that way. My parents took turns sharing their wisdom on how to take care of himself. Mark came for the food, of course. I watched while everyone lined up at the door, leaving with full bellies and tearful condolences for Kayan's loss, wishing him a safe trip.

With everyone gone, I immediately started to clean up the kitchen; I wanted no reminder of this night in the morning. Kayan stepped between a stack of dishes and me.

"You have to talk to me, Lara."

No, not really, I thought. *You'll be on a plane tomorrow morning, and that will be that.*

Kayan took the dishes from me. "Please talk to me."

"It was a very nice party. Are you packed?" I asked.

He reached out and grabbed my face between his hands, forcing me to look into his eyes. "Fifty days. I'll be home in 50 days. Look, I have my ticket home." He reached for an envelope on the kitchen counter, holding up his passport and a plane ticket home.

I was working so hard not to fall apart. I wanted to give him my approval, but I just didn't have it in me!

"I know." Kayan ran over to the stereo and put a record on. It was Barry White, with his deep, sultry voice singing our song, "Never Gonna Give You Up." He grabbed me, holding me closely, dancing and singing the words in my ear. Oh, that husband of mine was good. Thoughts came flooding in of the first time we met, the two of us dancing on the beach and Kayan announcing we now had our song.

I looked up at him. "Hurry home."

I don't remember much about the day Kayan left. Standing three feet from the door to the plane, I knew I had to finally let him go, figuratively and literally; emotionally was the difficult part, but I didn't want our last moments together to be an argument. I didn't want there to be anything but the love we shared at this moment. Kayan pulled me to him and slipped something into my hand. It was the tasbih, the worry beads that had been his grandfather's.

"I promise nothing is going to happen. Take care of these for me." Kayan kissed me. I could feel his excitement about seeing his family.

I whispered in his ear, "I love you, Kayan Batmanglij. You come home to me, in one piece!"

He whispered in my ear, "Never gonna give you up."

Two stewardesses opened the large doors to the plane. People rushed to board. It was all so surreal. I watched as Kayan dragged his green, oversized duffle bag towards the door—the same bag he had dragged into our apartment when we had first moved in together. Only now, it was filled with trinkets for his family from the United States. Kayan was the last to enter the plane, the doors closing behind him. I looked at the beads in my hand and rubbed them between my fingers. I felt nothing.

When I returned from the airport, Kayan's smell permeated the bedroom. I picked up his pillow and held it to my face, thinking of the hours prior to his departure when we made love.

I reached up and grabbed my stuffed dog off the tall shelf where he had placed him, remembering the safety I had always felt while holding the very worn stuffed dog. But not this time.

V

IRAQ INVADES IRAN

Kayan had promised he'd call when he got to Iran. He explained in order for him to call, he would have to go to the phone company in the city, and even then, it was difficult to make outgoing calls.

Every day I waited for that phone call, and every time the phone rang and someone else said hello, my heart sank. Now I knew how Kayan felt while waiting for his family to call. I had become Kayan, and I hated it!

The first call I got was a week after he arrived. Kayan didn't sound like his normal upbeat self. It was understandable, but he was also being elusive, as if he couldn't talk. I hung up wanting more but reassured myself by focusing my attention on counting down the days until he would be home and our life would be back to normal. I also wrote to him every night on prepaid international stationary. It was one thin piece of blue paper; you would write on one side and, like an origami puzzle, fold it into a letter, licking the sides to seal it. Every morning I would drop the letter into the mail. It was my way of keeping the connection, and somehow it helped. The few times Kayan wrote back, the content was brief and more informational than anything. It was obvious he was uncomfortable with talking, but he did share how difficult things were in Iran and that it was not at all like the country he had left.

I would later learn the apprehension in his writing was because the government had made it a practice to search through mail and listen to phone conversations. They were watching everyone. No one was to be trusted. The threat of another coup was part of the daily reality.

On day 42 of Kayan's time in Iran, he called. I was so excited, I started going on about how soon he would be coming home when he stopped me.

"Lara, they won't let me out of the country!"

I stood there in silence with too many thoughts, unable to pull one out and put it into a sentence.

"Iraq has just invaded Iran and all the borders have been shut down. We're at war, Lara! I'm so sorry. I miss you so much!"

I angrily answered, "But you have a visa, you have your plane ticket home. How can they do that?"

We were both in tears. I could tell Kayan's head was spinning, trying to think of a way out. He was good at that. He was always creating other ways to do things, like when he needed to change colleges and his student visa said he couldn't. He hadn't skipped a beat and had gone to work on finding a way, which he did.

"I can try to sneak across the Turkish border," Kayan said, running the thought by me.

"Kayan, that sounds dangerous." What was I saying? He was smack dab in the middle of another war!

"This is not going to be over soon, Lara. Iraq crossed the border because they think the new regime in Iran is weak. They're fighting for Iran's oil."

There was so much to try to absorb in that conversation, all of it beyond my understanding. After that call, Kayan and I lost all contact with each other. With the new war there was even less information coming out of Iran. The news on the television began televising bits and pieces of the Iraq/Iran war. Iran had gone from being an unknown country to being the major headline throughout the world. "War!"

Farzad and Hamid tried to find out what was going on in Iran, but they had the same problem. It seemed the whole country had shut down. After three months I stopped counting days and started counting months. I didn't share much with my family or friends. They would ask about Kayan, then give me that sad look one gives when they feel pity. Some even talked about Kayan as if he was no longer with us.

I chose to live in denial. I refused to believe that anything bad could happen to him. It was emotionally safer than living in my real world. My biggest fear was that Kayan had been killed and that, without a way to communicate, I would never know. But that was my secret. I chased it out of my mind constantly, fearing that if I allowed it to take root, it would become true. Instead, I continued to write to Kayan every night, sharing all the silly things from that day, convincing myself he would be home soon.

My daily life continued—work, school, and an occasional event out of obligation. I didn't like going out or trying to be social. The questions were so hard to answer because there were no answers, leaving nothing but judgment from others.

One day I arrived home to hear voices coming from inside my apartment. If they were robbers, they were having a great time. I slowly opened the door, making sure to stay on the front porch. Inside were the makings of a party. A surprise party. With family and friends busy blowing up balloons and putting up a sign that read, "Happy Birthday Lara." I slowly closed the door and took a step back off my porch, trying to avoid the whole happy scene.

"Oh no, get in there." Mark walked up behind me, grabbed my arm, and dragged me into the apartment. For the first time in six months, my apartment was filled with laughter and happy energy. Who was I to deny the experience?

Debbie and Susan hugged me. "Happy birthday, Lara!" they both called out. Debbie whispered in my ear, "We miss you."

I tried to smile back. "Me too." Seemed like the proper thing to say.

My dad walked up behind me. "Shouldn't have given your mom a key to your apartment, kid." I turned and hugged him, watching my mother flit around the room laying out trays of food.

In the middle of the dining room table was a stack of Kayan's school belongings that I had long ignored. Everyone was making a concerted effort to work around them as if it was a shrine. I turned to my insensitive brother, who had his purposes in life.

"Mark, can you do me a favor? Move those things off the table and put them in the corner?"

With a sandwich dangling from his mouth, Mark nodded and dragged the items, dropping them in the corner. Everyone was silent, waiting for my reaction to Mark's brashness. I patted him on the shoulder and grabbed a sandwich.

The party was an opening for me; it reminded me how much I missed my life. After that, I consciously made an effort to stop mourning the loss of Kayan. I sucked at it. The not knowing if he was dead or alive was emotionally wrenching, so I did the best thing I knew to do: I surfed. I always took my problems to the ocean. I'd paddle out, chase all the thoughts from my mind, and focus on catching my favorite wave for the day; there was always a favorite...

Nothing changed in the Middle East. The war between Iraq and Iran continued. It was covered on all the news channels with footage of the battles being fought between the two countries. I feared that every dead or wounded body they showed would be Kayan. There was no news about anything stopping on either side. Fortunately, when the Shah had been in power, he had spent all the country's resources building up Iran's army. They had the finest in tanks, planes, and weapons. Iran was far from being weak.

The American hostage situation remained the same as well. Ted Koppel would give his report every night on Nightline, counting down the days. On January 20, 1981, after 444 days of being held, their captors released the American hostages. The release took place on the same day that Jimmy Carter left the White House and Ronald Reagan was sworn in as the new President of the United States. The captors wanted to send a message to the world that they were in control. Somehow, I thought maybe this change of events would help Kayan come home if he was still alive.

It would be another three months before I would hear from him.

The time definitely did not fly by. When the call did come in, all I could do was cry on the other end. He was alive! Although I'd denied it, I'd feared he had been killed. It was the only explanation I had as to why I hadn't heard from him.

"Lara, are you okay? I'm so sorry."

"You're alive," I blurted out mixed with sobs.

"Yes, I'm alive. I miss you so much." I didn't feel missed. All those months with no word didn't make me feel missed or loved. I dropped to the floor, feeling the unsteadiness of my legs. "Are you there, Lara? Can you hear me?"

"I thought you were dead," I answered.

"I went to war fighting the Iraqis with my brother Sergis. I didn't want to tell you; I knew you'd be scared."

"You went to war?"

"I didn't want to go, but Sergis insisted he was going, and I couldn't just sit home doing nothing while he went off to fight."

I was filled with a year's worth of anger. "Yes, you could! You are a college student and live in California with a wife who's home waiting for you and afraid you're dead! You didn't have to go and fight in a war that you have no place being in and leave me not knowing if my husband was amongst the piles of bodies they show on the news. Yes, you could!" It took everything in me not to slam down the phone, but knowing it could be the last time I would ever hear his voice again, I went silent instead.

"You're right, Lara, you have every right to never speak to me again. I didn't know what to do when Sergis said he was going to fight the Iraqis. I tried everything to stop him. My mother was hysterical. She didn't want to lose another son. So, I told her I would go and take care of him, but I didn't, I didn't take care of him!"

Kayan began crying. As much as I wanted to continue on my tirade, I stopped myself. This was not my strong husband on the other end of the line.

"Sergis is dead, Lara. It should have been me, I'm the oldest son. I was his big brother. I didn't take care of him, and now he's dead!" Kayan sobbed into the phone. I could tell he had been holding on to the pain for some time, so I listened until I thought he would hear my words.

"It wasn't supposed to be you, Kayan. I hate hearing you say that. How could you leave me not knowing if you were alive or dead? How could you?"

"I thought it would hurt you less if you didn't know the truth, Lara."

I didn't know how to respond. Maybe he was right. How much more would I have worried knowing he had gone off to fight in the war? I took a few deep breaths between my sobs as little bits of the anger started to fall away.

"It's not your fault your brother was killed, Kayan. He did what he wanted to do."

"Something really strange happened, Lara. The night before we went to fight, I had a dream that Sergis was killed fighting in front of me. That morning I told him about the dream, but he laughed at me. That day when we were fighting, Sergis was killed, just like in my dream. I should have stopped him. Do you think he's in heaven, Lara?"

Kayan's words were paralyzing. I knew he had just asked me a question, but I couldn't pull together my thoughts to give him an answer.

"Lara, are you there?"

"Yes, he's in heaven," I blurted.

Kayan knew I didn't believe in anything but heaven. He got the answer he wanted. What I really wanted him to know was that Sergis had made his choice, just like his brother Ali. They chose how they wanted to live their lives, and although the outcome of their choices was incredibly sad, no one could change what they chose to do—not even their big brother.

"I promised my mom I would bring back Sergis's body if anything happened. It was weeks before she found Ali."

Kayan continued to talk about his experience. It was horrific and beyond anything I could comprehend. I couldn't imagine my sweet and kind husband fighting on a battlefield. He had difficulty with a verbal argument.

"I want to come home, Lara." Finally, something was said that I could grasp. We both sobbed.

"Come home, Kayan," I responded.

"I miss you so much. Lara, I know I can never make it up to you for what I've done, but they still won't let me out of the country. They said maybe in the future they would give visas again, but not now, not while we're fighting with Iraq, and that could be years."

Kayan stopped speaking. There was silence, and then, from nowhere, he took the conversation to a place I had no preparation for. "The consulate said I can't leave the country, but they would give my wife a visa to come to Iran."

I didn't respond; I was still digesting his not knowing when he could ever leave Iran. I tried to understand what that meant for us. How long could I pretend to be happy, sitting and waiting?

"Did you hear me, Lara? I know it's not what we want, but we'd be together."

"I heard you," I answered, not sure what to say.

I ran different scenarios through my mind. Stay home and live my life unhappy without Kayan or take a chance at living with my husband in another country. But not just any country, one that had held Americans hostage and was currently at war.

"We'd be living in Tehran, nowhere near the border of Iraq where the fighting is. We'll be safe.

You'll be with me. I miss you so much, Lara."

I knew I had no time to think, not knowing when Kayan would be able to make another call.

"Yes, I'll come to Iran," I answered, and from that moment on we both became so excited knowing we were going to be together, the where became unimportant.

Getting a visa to go to Iran was surprisingly easy. Kayan went to the consulate in Tehran and was issued a visa for his wife to join him. He also sent me plane tickets for each leg of the trip, and just like that, I was going to Iran. My family was understandably against it, like I was against Kayan going. In fact, my father contacted the Iranian Consulate in Washington to see if he could stop it, but there was nothing they could do.

The ride to the airport with my parents was extremely uncomfortable. This was their only shot at stopping me. I knew I would have reacted the same way if I was in their shoes, but I wasn't. My shoes were dance shoes. In my head, I was already with Kayan and our lives were in bliss. It was just a different location, I told myself. Of course, in my heart, I was hoping to relocate; Iran was a temporary situation, and as soon as Kayan could get a visa out, we would return home.

"Lara, we don't think you are being rational. We don't want to see our daughter on Nightline!"

I acknowledged my father's words with a nod.

"You're using your heart, not your head, Lara. We love Kayan, but we also love our daughter," my mother pleaded. My mom had a way of evoking emotion when she talked to me. She was a master at it. However, it wouldn't work this time. My mind had already taken me to the next chapter with Kayan and living in Iran.

I hugged and kissed my parents, and whispered "I love yous" to them before getting on a plane to begin my three-day journey to Iran.

VI

THE JOURNEY

After a 12-hour flight, my first stop would be England. I would spend one night in London before boarding a plane the following morning to Istanbul, Turkey. Then, I would spend one night in Istanbul before boarding a plane to Tehran, all formalities to me. I kept my itinerary and tickets for England and Turkey tucked in my pocket and habitually checked on them, afraid they would somehow disappear if I didn't. I was counting each leg of my journey. I was in control. I had this.

My first night in London was uneventful. I was happy there was not a language barrier to overcome, but I still felt I needed an interpreter. I knew they were speaking English, but I couldn't understand a word and found myself tilting my head like a puppy, trying to grasp what was being said. Early the following morning, I took a shuttle to London's Heathrow airport for my 3-½ hour flight to Istanbul. The first thing I noticed was that the size of the plane was considerably smaller than any other I had ever been on, and it was packed! The second thing I couldn't help but notice was that the plane was filled with cigarette smoke. A gray haze hung in the air, covering everything in sight. The third thing I noticed was that I was the only person like me. The other passengers seemed to be mostly Middle Eastern, most likely from Turkey, and almost all were men. Many wore business suits, which made sense since Istanbul was so close to England.

Being with Kayan, I had become used to being around people from the Middle East and found the culture to be extremely polite and gracious. Every eye turned in my direction, and silence like a wave slowly moved through the plane. There I was, standing in front of them, blonde, dressed in California casual—USC sweatshirt, bell-bottom jeans, a blue backpack over one shoulder—and pushing the most adorable powder blue Samsonite suitcase down the aisle. I got it. This was my first experience as a minority outside my country, but it would not be my last.

I looked at the ticket in my hand while standing in front of two seats. A tall, lanky young man was seated in the aisle seat, trying to pretend I wasn't there. I showed him the number on my ticket and pointed to the window seat next to him. We said nothing. He looked at my suitcase and reluctantly stood up.

I extended my hand and said, "Lara," pronouncing my name slowly. We shook hands.

"Cyrus." A big smile covered his face. It was obvious he didn't need me to slow my speech for him to understand.

"You speak English," I announced.

Cyrus nodded. "Let me help you." He grabbed my suitcase and shoved it in an overhead compartment while I moved to the window seat.

"I'm sorry, I wasn't expecting you to speak English," I said.

"I just graduated from Minnesota State," Cyrus said as he sat down next to me.

"Where are you going?" I asked.

"I should be asking you that question. I'm going back to my country, Iran. I just finished my engineering degree, and I'm going back to help rebuild the country."

I nodded in approval.

"If you don't mind my asking, why are you going to Turkey?" Cyrus waited for my answer.

"Oh, I'm not. I'm going to Iran, too."

Cyrus looked me dead in the eyes. I knew he needed an explanation. "My husband is from Iran and is waiting for me. He lost two brothers during the fighting. He can't get out, but they will let me in, so here I am." That synopsis seemed to satisfy most, but not this guy.

"I'm surprised you got a visa," Cyrus said.

I proudly pulled out my passport and handed it to Cyrus, showing him where the Iranian Consulate in the United States had stamped my passport to enter Iran.

"Iran is nothing like the United States," he added.

I waited for the words, the words I had heard so many times from family and friends about the safety, or lack of it, for me in Iran. Before those words could come, I spoke. "I'll be fine. I'll be with my husband."

I noticed a textbook popping out of Cyrus's backpack. It reminded me of one afternoon on my college campus. I'd been seated on the lawn with an open book next to my backpack, but my attention was on the beauty of the clouds above me and then on Kayan, who had strutted over.

"Hey, you, you got a boyfriend?" Kayan yelled loud enough for others to hear. Students passing by looked at him nervously. He loved messing with people. "You heard me; you got a boyfriend?" he asked again.

I looked up at him, the sun in my eyes. "Yeah, I got a boyfriend, and you'd better scat. He's very jealous."

Kayan plopped down next to me and gave me a long kiss. Everyone around us was watching. He loved it. "I bet he is. Come on, let's switch this place!" Kayan stood up, reached down for my hand and pulled me to my feet. I laughed.

"It's ditch, let's ditch this place." Kayan gave me a blank look. I shook my head. "Never mind." I shoved my book into my backpack and handed it to him. Kayan bent down so I could hop on his back and away we charged down the center of the quad, holding our arms out like we were planes flying.

"Are you planning on living with your husband in Iran or returning to the States?" Cyrus asked. The words brought me back to the plane and Cyrus. He was waiting for the answer to a question I had not heard.

I didn't want to leave my thoughts, but Cyrus's stare told me he was set on getting his answer. "I'm sorry, what did you say?"

"Are you planning on staying in Iran or going back to the States?" Cyrus asked again.

"We're not really sure. We'd like to go back to the States, but right now Iran won't let him out—not without a new visa, which they say could take years."

Cyrus nodded. Anyone tied to Iran understood the difficulties going on inside the country. He and I talked nonstop for the rest of the flight, mostly about our expectations of what we'd see in Iran. Even though Cyrus had grown up there, he wasn't sure what would be left of the country he remembered, but he was determined to take his new engineering skills and put them to use in building a better Iran. My expectations were much simpler and consisted of rejoining my husband. The rest of the pieces were secondary.

During our conversation, we realized we both had tickets on the same flight with British Airlines to Tehran for the next day. I had a room reservation at the Sheraton in Istanbul that night for the layover. Cyrus figured he'd wing it and find a place for the night. Guys travel differently. For a moment I struggled with that male/female thing, which actually lasted half a minute.

"Maybe they have a room at my hotel. It's a little pricey. I didn't know of anywhere else to stay, but it's only for one night."

Cyrus shrugged. "I can check and see."

A woman with an English accent announced over the intercom we would be landing in Istanbul shortly. I looked out the window, expecting to see something that looked Turkish, whatever that meant.

VII

ISTANBUL

On the ground, armed military soldiers could be seen patrolling. They quickly scattered as our plane bounced down the sparsely paved runway. Takeoffs and landings were always my favorite part of flying, but not this time. The plane seemed to want to take off again rather than land. It jerked from side to side, throwing the passengers around with each jerk. Cyrus bounced into me. I bounced into him. Apologies came from each of us with each bounce.

As the plane rolled to a stop, I could see outside workers pushing a large set of stairs up to the plane. We were let out onto the runway. Up until then I had always walked into an airport with polished floors and murals on the walls. But this airport looked more like a military base and made me feel uneasy. I wasn't used to seeing soldiers carrying guns, and here it seemed matter-of-fact. There were no pretty buildings or friendly faces to greet you. Not exactly the friendly skies I was used to. I told myself that none of it mattered; I was on the last stop of my trip before seeing Kayan.

A long tram pulled up in front of the passengers and took us to a bunker-type building. It was all steel and completely open at one end, where we were herded in-side. There was a large military presence. Soldiers were mixed in with the passengers. They looked at us like we were the enemy and had all smuggled ourselves into their country.

Without saying a word, Cyrus and I immediately buddied up. A group of soldiers approached, barking with heavy Turkish accents, "Passport!" Cyrus held out his passport and I did the same. It seemed our mere presence had angered them in some way. Seeing rifles slung over the soldiers' shoulders took away any feel-ing of excitement we'd had before landing. Like two scared rabbits, we stood there wide-eyed, taking in the environment we had just found ourselves in. The soldier snatched the passport out of Cyrus's hand, then looked at me. I realized he feared me as much as I feared him. That was odd. I'd never known anyone to fear me. I slowly handed the soldier my passport; just as slowly he took it, turned, and marched away.

We watched while several other soldiers circled around the one with our passports, others adding themselves to the mix. Within minutes the disappointed soldier returned and handed the passports to Cyrus, never looking in my direction. He then turned on his heel and marched off. We both sighed with relief. Even though we didn't know what the threat was, we knew it was gone.

With all the commotion I hadn't realized that my suitcase, which had been at my side, was missing. I panicked and spun around, looking in all directions. "My suitcase is gone!"

Cyrus looked at the floor around him. "Mine's gone, too!" He flew into a panic, quickly moving from place to place inside the terminal. His height gave him an edge. As he looked over the crowd, I surveyed the hands of strangers, hoping my suitcase would be in one of them. Cyrus yelled, "I can't lose my bag!"

That made me think: What could be in this almost-stranger's bag? Maybe he was a drug runner and was using me as his cover? What did I know of this man? Anyone could see I would make a lousy mule! And then I saw it—my baby blue Samsonite suitcase moving in the crowd, without me!

"Cyrus, someone's stealing our bags!" I pointed to a man dressed in fatigues, walking away with both our bags. Like lightning, Cyrus took off after the man. I was close behind, yelling for the thief to stop. Cyrus grabbed the thief by the shoulder and spun him around. The thief seemed shocked by our reaction. Was he shocked because he had just been caught, or was the look upon his face disappointment in losing out on whatever treasures he thought we had? The thief did not understand a word we were saying to him.

Soldiers surrounded us again. This time they would surely save us from a criminal like this. The thief and Cyrus spouted their stories to the soldiers. The same soldier who wouldn't look me in the eyes now seemed perplexed by the whole situation. I grabbed our bags from the thief and stood defensively. The thief pleaded to the soldier. I was sure he was asking for mercy.

For the first time, the soldier looked me in the eyes. He was solemn. "His job to take bags to the street for you." The thief motioned to the bags and to the street outside.

"He's a luggage porter?" I asked.

Cyrus and I stood there, not knowing whether to feel angry or guilty. The soldiers dispersed, laughing amongst themselves and leaving us with the "thief." "I guess we should give him a tip?" I suggested.

Cyrus shot me a look. "For taking our stuff?"

I reached into my purse, pulled out two one-dollar bills, and handed them to the embarrassed thief-turned-porter. He quickly took the bills and reached to grab our bags. Cyrus and I shook our heads no, snatched our suitcases, and headed to the streets where a barrage of taxis was waiting for their passengers. Two taxis rushed up to where we were standing. Each driver got out and grabbed a suitcase. It was a standoff. They stood looking at us, waiting for us to solve the tie. Cyrus stepped in, choosing the one holding his bag, the valuable mystery bag. I took my suitcase back from the other, now-disappointed driver.

The taxi ride was silent. Maybe it was nerves or maybe it was the pure insanity of chasing some guy we thought had stolen our belongings, but I suddenly broke out into laughter. Without saying a word, Cyrus joined in. I was sure our driver thought we were high on something as he looked in the rearview mirror, watching Cyrus and I rolling with laughter in the back seat of his cab.

"Sheraton?" the driver asked.

I nodded yes, his words sobering us up. I started looking out the window, taking in the sights of Turkey. There wasn't much to see; everything seemed old and rundown. There were local people on the streets, busy running from here to there, the last bit of daylight pushing them to move a little faster. I hadn't thought about Turkey or what I might see. In my mind, it was nothing more than a stopover. The driver pulled up in front of the Sheraton. It wasn't as grand as the one back home, but it had a familiarity to it that felt good.

Once inside, Cyrus and I went to check in, hoping they would have a room for Cyrus. It was the typical Sheraton, beautifully lit with crystal chandeliers, polished marble floors, and a definite upper-class clientele hustling about. Cyrus and I stood in the middle of it all, looking at the check-in counter. The woman behind the counter wore a Sheraton uniform and a silk scarf tightly wrapped around her head. I wouldn't have noticed, but it seemed out of place for an employee working at the Sheraton. To me, scarves were something my parents had worn back in the day. My mother had a drawer full of them in beautiful colors and soft silky fabrics. I couldn't remember seeing one on her head, or anyone else's. I had never really thought of the purpose of a scarf. The woman at the counter listened to our needs and left us to check on a room for Cyrus, which gave us time to absorb our new surroundings.

I noticed there were lots of women wearing scarves, not just employees. In Iran, after the new regime took over, most women had begun to wear what they called the *chador*, a robe-like garment that covers the body from head to toe. A portion of the fabric is used to cover the face, except for the eyes in order to see. All the recent photos and movies that had come out of Iran showed hundreds of women dressed in the chador. Kayan had explained this was primarily due to the new Islamic regime. Strangely enough, I was told the chador was a way of keeping men from lusting after women. That struck a negative chord with me, having been raised with the women's rights movement.

"You know, it has to be hot and uncomfortable to be draped in that tent. If men have a problem, they should be the ones to be made uncomfortable," I had lectured Kayan, who smiled and nodded, knowing he had no dog in this fight. Kayan never argued with my points of humanity. Maybe it was because he knew I was correct, or he feared the wrath of Lara. Either way, it was wise. Kayan lived with one foot in and one foot out of a country that had recently adopted many new philosophies that he didn't agree with but didn't have the freedom to object to.

"How long will you be staying?" the woman behind the counter asked on her return.

"One night. We both have a flight to Tehran tomorrow morning," I answered.

The woman shook her head no. "I have a room for the night, but there are no flights going to Tehran tomorrow. Not since the war broke out with Iraq. It's too dangerous to fly the planes."

I felt the blood rush through my body. What was this woman saying? Surely she was someone with no knowledge. Or maybe we were having a language barrier. Without skipping a beat, I opened my backpack and pulled out my ticket from British Airways. It clearly showed it was a ticket to Iran. Both Cyrus and I waved our tickets in front of this annoying woman.

The woman stood her ground, shaking her head no. "I'm sorry."

"Can you check with somebody?" Cyrus insisted.

Annoyed at the request, the woman stomped off. Cyrus and I found a place in the lobby to wait while she received the correct information. I was so adamant, not just because I didn't believe what she was saying, but more importantly because the reality of her truth paralyzed me with fear. I had no plan B. This was it. I had no "get out of Turkey free" card. Kayan wasn't going to be able to ride in on a white horse and save me. That was not going to happen. I had a ticket on British Airlines for the next morning. I would board the plane. My husband and his family would be waiting for me at the airport. I even had a traveling companion who had a ticket on the same flight. There was no reason for a plan B, I told myself, looking at the ticket in my hand.

After what seemed like forever, I could hear the woman behind the counter approaching by the click of her heels on the marble floor. I didn't want to turn and face this woman, who was not a nice person. Cyrus looked at her. No one said a word. The silence caused me to turn in her direction.

She was shaking her head no. "I'm sorry, there are no flights. You'll have to talk to British Airlines. Let me know what you want to do about the rooms." And she was gone.

I felt the tears starting to well up; I took a deep breath, hoping to hold them back. I didn't want Cyrus or anyone else to see me as weak. When I turned away, I noticed a nicely dressed woman standing off to the side, staring at us. I couldn't help but notice how meticulously she was dressed in her black pencil skirt and copper-colored scarf that looked like it had been glued to her head. She was partially hidden by a marble statue. A busybody no doubt. I nudged Cyrus, motioning to the woman. Cyrus glared back at her, the typical macho male challenging the nosy woman.

Rather than watch the showdown, I picked up my suitcase and moved to several couches that were perfectly situated for guests to feel at home. It was an illusion, a placebo; this did not feel like home. I sat down, trying to digest the situation, and came to the conclusion that we were screwed!

Cyrus approached. I didn't want to unload my anger and fear onto him, and as much as I wanted to fall apart, there was no time. Hiding out in the Sheraton was not an option. Neither of us could afford the luxurious hotel for very long, and my visa only gave me a few days to cross into Iran.

"I may be able to help." We slowly turned to see the woman who had been staring was now standing behind us.

We didn't say a word to the woman, which must have signaled to her that it was okay to approach. She moved to a chair not too close, giving the outward impression that we were not together but staying close enough for us to hear her. She looked away when we looked in her direction, again showing others we were not together. Cyrus and I were still in shock, trying to grasp our reality. We had no time for stalkers pretending to not be talking to us.

"I'm sorry, but I heard you want to get to Iran, yes?" she said in broken English.

She had asked the right question. Cyrus and I nodded yes.

"The lady at the counter is right, there are no flights. They are afraid the Iraqis will shoot down the planes. There are two more ways to cross into Iran."

Both Cyrus and I listened intently with new hope. Like a spy in a movie, the woman looked away from us. "There is a train that leaves Istanbul tonight at 8:00. It will take you one hour away from the border of Iran. You can take a bus from there. You must be very careful. We have martial law because of recent uprisings in Turkey. You cannot be on the streets after 8:00; you will be arrested."

Arrested? The movie *Midnight Train* ran through my mind. It was the story of a young American man who had gotten caught for drug trafficking and thrown into a Turkish prison. It was horrific.

"Lara, are you okay?"

I looked up at Cyrus. I wanted to say, "No, get me out of here," but with nowhere to turn, I just stared back.

"How many days will it take to get to the border by train?" Cyrus asked

The mysterious woman rocked her head side to side. "Two, maybe three, but you must be very careful." She lowered her already-low voice to a mere whisper. "Turkey is a very dangerous place for tourists, especially one who looks like you." The woman, who had avoided eye contact, now stared directly at me. "You must be very careful. There are thieves everywhere, thieves that will slit your throat for a piece of jewelry! Last week they found the body of a pregnant woman who had taken a taxi and was driven up to the hills, killed for her necklace. A necklace!" The woman sadly moved her head back and forth.

I looked at Cyrus, who was speechless. "You said there were two ways to reach the border?" I asked.

"You're a smart one. Yes, there is another way, a much better and faster way, but I have to ask my friend if he can help."

It was as if we were playing cat and mouse, and she was holding back the prize. She looked suspiciously around the lobby. I followed her stare, not knowing who or what we were looking for.

"I must be careful. I work in the gift shop here. I don't want anyone to hear me. I have a friend who has a taxi. He may be able to drive you to the border. You will be safe with him. Of course, he will charge you."

"How much?" Cyrus asked

"I will call him and let you know. Wait here in the lobby for me. Speak to no one."

We watched the mysterious woman stand up and slowly move away from us, fading into the crowd at the hotel. Something didn't feel right—the kind of thing that made the hair stand up on the back of your neck. Every ounce of my being was telling me to get away from this woman.

I looked up at Cyrus. "Let's get the hell out of here. We only have 20 minutes if we want to catch that train!"

Cyrus jumped to his feet. "You read my mind!"

We didn't understand why, but both of us were having the same reaction to this seemingly harmless woman. Getting away from her became just as important as catching the train.

"Wait, I need to call and tell my family. I have to let someone know where I am. Kayan will be waiting at the airport tomorrow!"

"We don't have time; we'll be lucky if we catch the train!" Cyrus said in a panic.

For a moment I paused, thinking about my family and Kayan. How could I disappear without them knowing where I was, or if I was okay? But the truth was, I wasn't okay. For the first time since I left home, I wasn't safe.

I looked up at Cyrus, who was nervously waiting for my response. I jumped to my feet. "Let's go find that train!"

VIII

THREE STRANGERS

Within minutes we were in a cab that we had cautiously picked with a driver who seemed to be the least likely to kill us. Cyrus kept looking at his watch.

"Are we going to make it, Cyrus?" I asked.

He didn't answer, just looked at his watch again. "Depends on how on time Turkish trains are."

That wasn't the answer I wanted to hear. He looked at his watch again. The streets were pitch black and the city had long disappeared. We were the only car on the road. We were uneasy about our fate, and that had nothing to do with catching a train and everything to do with our new circumstance.

Cyrus showed the driver his watch over and over again, as if that would get us there sooner. Each time, the driver would anxiously nod, acknowledging Cyrus's panic. And then, from out of nowhere stood a huge iron train that went on further than we could see. We had made it! Cyrus threw the driver a few dollars, not knowing the currency or the language. It made the driver happy. He smiled and hurried to help us with our suitcases.

"We haven't time. Give me your suitcase!" Cyrus shouted.

Before I could respond with, "I don't need anyone's help," Cyrus grabbed my suitcase and started running towards the train. I scrambled to catch up to him, his long legs making it a challenge. The train let out an ear-piercing whistle. Yelling and loud voices were coming from behind us, but we kept moving forward until we were surrounded by a group of armed Turkish soldiers with their rifles aimed directly at us.

"Passports." One of the soldiers held out his hand.

My mind immediately went numb. I had never been around guns. Fear told me to run, which would have obviously been the wrong choice. One of the soldiers gave me a grin. They were enjoying their moment of power. Cyrus struggled with his words, trying to communicate, but their eyes and guns were focused in my direction. I couldn't help but notice that the group of soldiers looked more like thugs than military. Their uniforms were dirty and in poor condition, faces unshaven and covered with black soot, making their eyes seem to pop out.

"Passports!" one ordered again.

I dropped my bags. "It's okay, Cyrus, let's give them what they want." I bent down and started rummaging through my backpack.

Cyrus dropped the suitcases and lowered his voice. "We don't have time."

"We don't have a choice," I whispered back.

One of the soldiers lowered the tip of his rifle towards my face. My hand began to shake as I handed over my passport. The train blew its whistle again and rocked a little harder. The conductor leaned out a window, yelling in Turkish. The soldier in charge examined our passports, like we were the enemy.

"We are going to Iran and we need to get on that train!" Cyrus spoke in broken Farsi and English. He motioned to the train that was now surrounded by smoke from the engine. The air around us took on a white, billowy appearance, like a Sherlock Holmes movie. It would have seemed funny, except for the fact that once ingested, it caused us to start choking. The soldier handed Cyrus back his passport, but held on to mine, like he was waiting for a ransom.

"You go to Iran?" asked the soldier.

"Yes, I have a visa." I pointed to my passport.

The soldier paused and slapped my passport in his hand. "Why you go to Iran? It's very dangerous for you. I don't go to Iran!" The soldier repeated what he was saying to the others in Turkish, and they all laughed. "You want to be hostage?" More laughter.

"I'm joining my husband in Iran. Please, let us go. We're going to miss the train!" I reached to take my passport.

Begrudgingly, the soldier looked at my passport and handed it back to me. "You'd better hurry, you have two days or visa no good. You can stay here with me!" A dirty sneer covered his face.

Cyrus grabbed me and practically lifted me onto the train. We both stood frozen, cautiously looking around us. Flickering lights gave off a strobe kind of effect— not exactly welcoming. A long, narrow walkway ran the length of the train. On one side were windows that looked out into the darkness of the night; on the other side there were cabins that were separated from the hallway by curtain-covered windows and wooden sliding doors. I could tell that at one time this old train had sparkled with polished hardware and rich woods, but that was many years ago. Now it looked shamefully neglected and abused.

Cyrus opened the sliding door of one of the cabins and poked his head in. Just as quickly, he closed the door and backed away.

"What's wrong?" I asked.

He seemed more anxious than ever, which I didn't question after what we had experienced so far. If I had been smarter, I would have been, too.

"I think we need to keep from attracting attention," he answered.

I unzipped my backpack and pulled out a black hooded sweatshirt. I slipped my arms inside and covered my hair with the hood, looking at Cyrus for approval. Cyrus said nothing, obviously uncomfortable addressing my wardrobe.

A cabin door suddenly opened and a young man in his twenties stepped out. Startled, he looked at us and walked away quickly. Cyrus glanced inside the cabin before pushing me inside. The cabin was barely lit. There were two bench seats that faced one another and a large window between them. A heavy smell of dust filled my lungs. A young man, maybe 19, was sitting comfortably inside. Casually, he looked up at us and jumped to his feet. Cyrus motioned for the young man to sit back down. I could tell the stranger was frightened, his eyes transfixed on the open door. He was ready to escape. I couldn't understand his reaction to us. Again, I wondered how we had become people to be afraid of.

Cyrus held out his hand to the young man, who had now slid down to the end of one of the bench seats. "I'm Cyrus, this is Lara." I could tell Cyrus was testing the waters, wanting to see if this young man was friend or foe.

"Parvis." Parvis shook Cyrus's hand and gave me a nod. Cyrus smiled approvingly and motioned for me to sit on the bench across from our new cabinmate. It appeared Parvis did not understand what was being said but had passed the cabinmate test. Cyrus nervously paced the cabin, peeking out through the thick, dark green curtains that hung on the windows leading to the outside hallway. He looked at me like a frightened tiger, not knowing what to do.

Calmly, I said, "Cyrus, we made it, we're good."

Cyrus looked around the cabin, then at me, before sitting down on the same bench as Parvis. "We made it." He repeated the words several times, convincing himself of their truth. Parvis watched us cautiously. We were definitely not your average passengers on this train.

The sliding door suddenly opened. We all jumped to our feet. It was the young man we had seen previously leaving the cabin. It was a standoff now, everyone staring at one another, not quite knowing how to react.

"Hello, my name is Lara." I extended my hand to our new guest, who politely shook my hand. "This is Cyrus." Reluctantly the two shook hands and introduced themselves. It was more like a roll call than an introduction.

"Omar," the man announced.

Omar had a round face with a boyish look. He was small in stature, and both he and Parvis were dressed nicely in slacks and shirts. Parvis had the beginnings of a mustache that hadn't quite grown or covered any part of his face; it was just a shadow, a reminder that he was still a boy.

Once everyone had sized each other up, Cyrus quickly tried to start up a conversation with our new friends. He motioned to Omar to take a seat next to Parvis before squishing himself next to them on the same bench seat, leaving me sitting alone. We quickly discovered they were Turkish and didn't speak English or Persian. It became quite amusing watching the three of them struggle to understand each other's stories. Cyrus was the most animated, maybe because he was the one that needed to communicate the most. It was like a game of charades, and when they guessed the other's words, there was immediate celebration.

Cyrus jumped over to the seat next to me. "They're students from Turkey on their way home to see their families. They said the train will take two days and will leave us an hour from the Iranian border. We can take a bus the rest of the way. They also said we will be safe on the train."

The word "safe" had become a red flag. Even if I didn't understand what the danger was, it didn't mean it didn't exist. Just like in *The Wizard of Oz*, it was obvious we were not in Kansas anymore. I forced a smile back at Cyrus. He was excited about his accomplishment and quickly returned to bonding with his new friends. I watched for a while, trying to figure out what story he was telling. When all eyes looked in my direction, I knew it was my story.

I wasn't comfortable sharing my life with people or strangers. I had to adjust to the fact that this was to become my new norm. Everyone wanted to know who the American girl traveling through the Middle East was. I wanted to know too, especially at a time when there was so much chaos and unrest. Cyrus seemed to enjoy telling my story. When he pointed to my wedding ring, the others sadly rocked their heads.

I looked at my ring, twisting it around my finger, my thoughts momentarily taking me back to Kayan and our life together. I thought if I just closed my eyes, I could be back there and all the craziness of the present would disappear. I closed my eyes and let the sound of the train tracks carry me back to the beaches of Malibu and Kayan trying to surf...

A loud bang from the cabin door shook the train cabin and everyone in it awake. We all sat dazed, looking at one another. Through the window we could see daybreak. Slowly, my attention was drawn to the cause of the noise.

Standing in the doorway were two huge male figures covered in dirty, loose-fitting white clothes with turbans wrapped around their heads and large swords tied at their waists. The swords were so big they actually dragged on the floor. I was frozen in my seat, taking in the sight of the men. One of them stared directly at me. His dark brown, weathered skin was covered with the same thick dust as the train. It covered every inch of him except for the glistening sword. Both men stepped towards me. I looked at my cabinmates. No one moved.

Then Cyrus stood up and was immediately shoved back down by one of the intruders. Omar started to nervously talk in Turkish. He talked fast, as if they were the last words he would ever speak. Parvis nodded his head, supporting everything that came from Omar. The two intruders had no reaction to anything that was being said. Omar's voice started getting louder and more excited. There was a pause as the intruders surveyed everyone in the cabin, finally resting their eyes on my ring. *Thieves*, I told myself.

Omar dropped to his knees and began to pray. "Allah, Allah, Allah!" Parvis and Cyrus joined Omar on the floor. Although the intruders had fixed their attention on me, the sight of these three grown men on the floor praying seemed to be distracting them. I didn't know whether to scream, run, or get down on the floor with everyone else. The worst part was not knowing what the threat was, or how fearful I should be. Was it a "my car is almost out of gas" kind of fear, or a "there's a knife at my throat" kind of fear? I was thinking the latter.

Looking at the swords and the panic they brought to the cabin, it became obvious the two ominous intruders were not friendly; they had everyone so frightened that they had turned to prayer. I looked at the intruders and did the best thing I knew to do: I prayed. I can't say what I prayed for, but I prayed with every ounce of my being.

For the first time, the two intruders spoke, in angry, deep, loud voices.

Omar softly spoke back. The standoff continued with the two intruders watching the three grown men in front of them vigorously praying. One of the intruders looked me directly in my eyes. I tried not to acknowledge him or the powerlessness and fear that I was feeling. Without turning, the intruders slowly backed out of the cabin.

We all stayed in our prayer positions, too frightened to see if they had actually gone. Finally Cyrus jumped to his feet, followed by Omar and Parvis. Cyrus cautiously looked out the window and down the train's hallway.

"Cyrus, what the hell was that about?" I asked.

"I have no idea, but I know we just got saved!" Cyrus started taking deep breaths, trying to calm himself.

Omar spoke anxiously, interspersing broken Turkish with bits of English, "Very bad men. They live there!" He pointed to the mountains beyond the vast desert, and then he pointed at me. "They hear young American woman on train. They come for you. They take you and you gone!"

My mind could not wrap itself around what was being said. "Why would they want me?" I asked.

Omar anxiously responded, "You, young American woman, blue eyes, light skin. You make valuable wife." Omar and Parvis nodded in unison.

"But I am a wife, and I have a husband."

Omar spoke up. "I tell them. I say, 'She wife to Muslim soldier in Iran. Allah would be very angry if she were taken from her husband.'"

"That's why they kept looking at my ring," I said.

"And why we kept praying to Allah," Parvis added.

Cyrus took more deep breaths, which didn't seem to be helping him.

Omar nodded. "It is true you are protected by Allah." He and Parvis looked upwards, holding their hands in prayer.

"I don't feel protected. What if they change their minds and decide to come back? Cyrus, I have to get off the train!" I jumped up, not knowing which way to move. Everyone stood up.

Omar stood in front of me, shaking his head no. "They go. They not come back. Allah protects you."

The sun was rising, and for the first time I could see where we were. Outside the window the landscape was vast and barren except for snow-covered mountains in the far distance. Being from Southern California, I always got a thrill from seeing snow, but this time I felt small and scared, and the saying, "out in the middle of nowhere" took on a whole new meaning. I could also see where the dust on the train had come from. The dry desert terrain went on endlessly for miles. I watched in amazement as cars whizzed past us on a desolate highway that ran parallel to the train tracks. If I hadn't been so anxious, I would have found humor in the sight. My feelings were overwhelming. What if they decided to come back?

I looked around the cabin at the three strangers waiting for me to do something. Somehow, they had become my saviors. I had never needed to be saved before, but I was grateful they were there. Feeling numb, I slid back into my seat.

The two days that followed were difficult. I kept myself covered with my sweatshirt and hood at all times. I had to adapt to my new role, challenges and all. I could never get off the train or gain attention in any way. When we stopped at a train station, Omar and Parvis would exit to get us food and something to drink while I would move away from the window.

I had always been a modest person, and now, in front of three men, I had to announce that I needed to use the restroom. It went like this: Cyrus would leave the cabin first, scoping out the halls and restroom. Omar and Parvis would become lookouts along the way. A knock on the cabin door meant it was safe for me to go. I would fly down the halls to the bathroom where Cyrus would stand outside guarding the door. I made a point of drinking and eating very little, which had nothing to do with my modesty, but rather had to do with the bathroom itself. It was a small, filthy box with a hole in the floor that went straight through to the tracks!

Funny how quickly I had gone into survival mode. I was surprised that I had one, but it was like awakening a beast that consumed all my thoughts and movements. I told my Pollyanna self to get smart and quick! Omar and Parvis were very helpful, too; I couldn't ignore the serendipity that they, like Cyrus, had shown up in my life before I even knew I needed them.

Besides food, Omar would always pick up a newspaper and share with us what was going on in the country. Turkey happened to be in the throes of a rebellion with its government. There were demonstrations against the leadership, and the government had come down harshly, implementing martial law.

The next afternoon, when the train made a stop, Omar and Parvis got off to get a newspaper. We knew we were getting close to our destination and wanted to make sure there would be no surprises waiting for us at the border. The thought of crossing into Iran was exciting. Both Cyrus and I were looking forward to bringing this part of our journey to an end. We remained on the train and, like always, I moved away from the window to avoid being seen by someone outside.

The cabin door opened. I looked up expecting to see our friends, but instead saw a police officer. We were both shocked at the sight of each other. I'm sure he wished he had simply turned around and left, but he didn't.

"Passports!" he bellowed. Cyrus and I handed over our passports.

"Coca-Cola!" Omar entered the cabin waving bottles of coke and a newspaper in the air. He froze at the sight of our guest. A long, heated discussion in Turkish ensued between the officer and Omar.

"You go to Iran tomorrow?" the officer asked me.

"Yes," I eagerly nodded. The frustrated officer handed Cyrus our passports and marched out.

Omar and Parvis laughed quietly. "He told us we should be in school, not riding trains with foreigners," Omar shared.

Learning to survive in my new world was quite different from my middle-class upbringing in the United States. Unlike the United States, the Middle East does not have a multitude of cultures living together. It was this simple fact that made my being there so difficult and why I stood out. In Turkey, standing out made me easy prey for unscrupulous characters. I'm sure if I had been a man, it would not have been as much of an issue.

Later that day we pulled into a large train station in the city of Alborz, the home of both Omar and Parvis. Saying goodbye wasn't easy. Omar and Parvis took their responsibility for our safety seriously and personally. It was surprising how close we had all become in such a short amount of time. Survival had bonded us in a very powerful way, but we didn't exchange contact info. It was an accepted fact that we would never see one another again. This had been a life's experience, a moment in time shared by four strangers: three who took it upon themselves to protect a young American woman crossing Turkey. For that, I am eternally grateful.

IX

THE FIVE-STAR GENERAL

The next day Cyrus and I reached the end of the line on the train. We planned to take a bus to the Iranian border the following morning. Getting off the train was liberating and scary at the same time. The train had become our sanctuary, but we were well aware we were still in Turkey. We anxiously looked forward to crossing into Iran and putting the frightening past behind us.

Because we had taken the train instead of the plane, my visa was in jeopardy of expiring the following day. Fortunately, Cyrus found there was an Iranian Embassy in the little town due to its close proximity to the Iranian border.

The embassy was a small office, hardly noteworthy. From the outside, it looked more like an insurance building. Obviously, Iran's embassy held little importance in Turkey. Cyrus approached the receptionist and requested to see someone to help us extend my visa. Without looking up, the woman handed him a sign-in sheet.

"Thank you," I responded.

It felt good to see another woman, even though she didn't look like any woman I had ever seen. She was covered in a traditional black chador. The receptionist quickly covered her face with the hanging fabric and looked up at me. Without saying a word, she sprinted to a door behind her and entered. The door she entered was very ornate, with hand carvings of kings on horses and a bronze plaque with Persian writing that looked as if it said, "The person behind this door is important."

Cyrus looked down at me and shrugged while signing us in. "How do you spell your last name?" he asked.

"It's Batmanglij, one word."

Cyrus looked at me. It was my turn to shrug.

The receptionist returned, snatched the incomplete sheet from Cyrus, and had us follow her into another office. Sitting behind a desk was a very heavyset man wearing a dark suit that pulled at the seams. It was obviously purchased when he was a slimmer version of himself. He looked up at us from behind his glasses.

If he had been in a different setting, I'm sure he would have sworn. Instead, he jumped up and motioned to two French provincial chairs in front of his desk. "Please sit. Tea?"

Cyrus jumped at the opportunity to have something hot and not named Coca-Cola. The receptionist hurried out the door after she was given the drink order. I could tell the man was powerful and of importance to her.

"Ali," Ali announced himself and shook Cyrus's hand.

"Cyrus Abedini." That was the first time I had ever heard Cyrus's last name. All this time we had spent together, and we hadn't known each other's last names.

Ali extended his hand to me. "Mrs. Abedini."

Before I could correct him, Cyrus stepped in and, speaking in Persian, explained our situation. Ali sat back down behind his desk and listened. I handed Ali my passport. The receptionist returned with a tray of three small, clear cups of tea. I was not in a tea party mood but had learned long ago that when offered something by someone who was Persian, you'd best accept it with a smile. If not, they would insist on finding something that they could give you to make you happy.

Cyrus was in heaven, sipping his tea and clearly feeling normal for the first time in a long time. However, poor Ali didn't know what to do with his unexpected guests. I was impatient, but knowing what the accepted protocol was, I calmly sipped the tea so we could move on to the reason we were there.

"Can you extend my visa to make sure I can cross the border tomorrow?" I asked, hoping Ali understood my English.

Ali looked at me and spoke in a fatherly voice. "I know you want to be with your husband; you've already come so far. I am worried about your safety with Iran being at war and the American hostages having just been released."

Did he really think I was going to turn around and go home? Or that his wise fatherly words would change my mind about being with my husband?

I paused, looking at Ali, reminding myself I needed his help. "If I could just get an extension for another day or two..." I said.

Reluctantly, Ali opened my passport and stamped it with a large, ornate stamp that looked like something royalty would use to allow you safe passage. I guess that's what it was. Slowly, he rose from his desk chair and walked around to hand it to me.

"You have two days to cross into Iran."

I took the passport. "Thank you!"

It was becoming evening by the time we left the Iranian Consulate; we knew it would be too late to cross the border, which opened at eight in the morning and closed at five in the evening. We would take a bus to cross the border first thing in the morning, then board another bus in Iran that would take us to Tehran. Both Cyrus and I were beyond happy to be leaving Turkey.

We decided we would have to get a hotel room for the night. For a miniscule moment there was that awkward pause again. After all, we were a woman and a man sharing a hotel room. How would I explain that to my husband? The conversation would go something like this: "That airline ticket you bought me, Kayan, didn't work because of a silly thing called war and the threat of my plane being shot down! Fortunately, I met this wonderful person who was on his way to Iran as well. Together we've had guns aimed at us, threats against our lives, and oh yes, bandits with swords jumped our train to take me to be their wife or sell me. We didn't get the whole story."

I looked up at Cyrus. "You're in charge of getting us a room." I spent what seemed like hours in the bathroom showering off all the soot and dust from the train. I also hadn't seen my reflection for days. I had a weary, drawn look and darkness around my eyes that wasn't familiar to me, but I knew how it had gotten there. After the experience with our visitors on the train, I'd kept myself awake, too afraid to relax into sleep.

While I was cleaning up, Cyrus had gone out and gotten food—real, hot food. Up until now the only thing we had eaten was flat bread brought to us by Omar and Parvis. Our room was simple, with two twin-size beds, a small chair, and white linens, which gave it a clean feeling. Sleeping that night was difficult, but it had nothing to do with fear or the room. It was the excitement that we were finally going to cross into Iran!

The early hour didn't bother us the following morning when we got on a bus that would take us to the Turkish border. Knowing we were only an hour away from Iran was all that mattered. The bus itself was just as dusty as the train and was filled with laborers, mostly men dressed in work clothes still covered in the soil from their week's work. Some carried toolboxes.

As the bus approached the border, we could see an endless line of people waiting to cross. The line was mostly made up of men. There were a few families with impatient children swinging on their arms.

When we exited the bus, every person standing in line looked in our direction. We stood there awkwardly, trying to figure out where to go. A man from the bus motioned for us to join him at the end of the line. We dragged our luggage with us, making sure not to take our eyes off our bags. It was impossible to see where the line ended or where it would take us, but we happily took our place at the end knowing we were feet away from our destination.

The border crossing resembled a fort with 40-foot-high walls that made it impossible to see anything beyond them. Armed soldiers hurried about, all with a look of official duty on their faces. Above the wall were more soldiers looking down onto the crowds of people. Barbed wire fences were mixed in, keeping people where they wanted them and away from where they didn't. There was a huge wall of heavy stone and metal gates, and a bridge above lined with more armed soldiers, their sights set on the people below, including us. Their guns unnerved me. The mere sight made me shiver. You would think I'd be desensitized by now, but I wasn't.

It seemed my existence was creating quite a stir at the border, too. Several soldiers approached us, some with coats covered with an assortment of military medals. They all looked angry and upset.

"Passport!" one soldier barked at me. I knew the drill by now and kept my passport close. Cyrus handed him his passport as well and once again started telling my story in Persian. One soldier moved in to interpret, speaking both Turkish and Persian.

At this point I accepted that I had lost much of my independence and needed my translator not just for language; without Cyrus, I was barely acknowledged at all. Most looked away, partially because I was a woman in a man's world, but mostly because I was an American woman in the Middle East. The need to dominate was obvious. I was shown little to no respect as an individual. If I had a need, they would address Cyrus, but not me. It was definitely fear-based in many ways. I had a lot of power. Just looking at me made people nervous— a very different role for me. How I would handle it was yet to be seen.

In the meantime, I had this amazing stranger, Cyrus, who was put in my life for a reason. For Cyrus, traveling with me had turned out to be a full-time job. He and I had become friends the moment we shared our stories with each other. How that happened I do not know, but if ever there was a synchronicity moment, that was it. Neither Cyrus nor I ever questioned our roles in each other's journey.

I opened my passport for the soldier to see and showed him the new stamp inside. Why did I think that it mattered? It didn't. The officer snapped up my passport and abruptly marched away, followed by his entourage. There was a rustle that came from the people waiting in line with us. It had become obvious they feared the soldiers through the deafening silence when they had approached. After the soldiers left, the people were buzzing with conversation, like bees in a hive. Cyrus was able to speak to the other Persians in line.

"What are they saying?" I asked. It hadn't gone unnoticed that mine was the only passport that was being asked for.

Cyrus looked down at me in a consoling way. "It will be okay. They said there's a five-star general here today, and everyone is trying to impress him."

"I'm ruining it, aren't I?"

Cyrus nodded. "They know you are here."

Before we could get used to our new spots in line, the soldier who had taken my passport returned with a small-armed army. He motioned for us to follow him. Part of me thought maybe this would get us across the border faster, the other feared they had found a reason to not let me cross their border.

There was a tremendous amount of energy around us. People were moving quickly all about and several soldiers were taking our suitcases. I knew not to argue. We were led to a single-story cinderblock building, where we were instructed to separate from each other. I looked up at Cyrus. I could see the concern in his eyes. "I'm okay, just remember where you left me." I gave him my reassuring smile. This was the first time we had been separated in four days. We watched each other being whisked away in different directions.

The room I was taken to had several women dressed in chadors. Without saying a word, they instructed me to hand them my shoes and partially undress. My modesty kicked in big time, but I could also sense their discomfort as well. Somehow that made the experience more tolerable. Intellectually, I understood what was going on. At that moment I was seen as a possible threat, whether it be drugs, weapons, or a bomb hidden on my person. Everyone needed to feel safe, especially that five-star general.

The women asked me to hold my arms out to the sides. One of the women patted me down and, with much discussion, I was found to be free of anything dangerous and was left alone in the room. Wanting to know my fate, I tried to listen and understand the conversations going on outside the door, but without being able to read the expressions on their faces, it was futile. I was still on the Turkish side of the border, and anything being spoken was most likely in Turkish.

There was a part of me that worried about Cyrus. I hoped he wasn't being punished for being with me. Different thoughts played in my mind, none of them pleasant. I wished I had been left in that long line like everyone else. I was tired of standing out. I was tired of everyone's attention being fixed on me. What I wouldn't give to blend…

"Lara, are you all right?" Cyrus's voice came from somewhere beyond the walls of the room I was sitting in.

"I'm okay. Cyrus, are you okay?"

There was silence. My imagination raced. Could they be torturing him? Was he being used to get information about the scary American?

The door flew open. A barrage of soldiers entered and motioned for me to follow them. Outside the room I could see Cyrus sitting on a bench against a wall, looking like a child being disciplined in the principal's office. He stood up and was led by soldiers to join me. We were escorted out of the building and into the courtyard, where armed gunmen watched from above. The line of people waiting to cross the border seemed not to have moved one bit. Perhaps we were the holdup.

Buses packed with passengers rolled into the courtyard and lined up in front of us. Standing alone in the courtyard with the soldiers above aiming their guns down at us, I felt as if we were in a firing squad. In the distance I could see what all the fuss was about.

A soldier in a well-pressed uniform, with badges, buttons, and medals covering almost every inch of his jacket, stood watching us. The feared five-star general! He looked more like a king than a military man. His rigid stance and superiority flowed from his being. He owned his five-star stature.

The general handed something off to one of the men standing next to him, who handed it off to someone else, who handed it off to another. Finally, the last man receiving it marched over to the soldiers surrounding us. The item being handed off was our passports. One of the soldiers watching us took the passports and handed them to Cyrus. We had passed their test! Our luggage was brought out and placed on the ground in front of us. A team of soldiers opened up Cyrus's duffle bag and pulled its belongings out onto the ground. Carton after carton of Marlborough cigarettes tumbled out. Cyrus didn't smoke—at least, I had never seen him smoke— and yet there must have been at least 20 cartons of cigarettes lined up for all to see, one right after the other.

My paranoia kicked in. Was it illegal to have so many cigarettes? Were we now smugglers? Who was this stranger I had been traveling with? Between the armed soldiers on the bridge and now more than 20 cartons of possible contraband laid out on the ground, I felt a meltdown coming on. I looked up at Cyrus for an explanation. He shrugged. I couldn't believe he'd just shrugged!

"They're gifts for my family; cigarettes are very expensive in Iran."

We suddenly became more interesting to the soldiers around us. They turned their attention to my suitcase, which had now been placed on the dirty ground. The same soldier who had initially opened Cyrus's bag was now unsuccessfully attempting to open my suitcase. He looked up at me. With everything going on, I had forgotten I had locked it.

Without thinking, I grabbed my backpack off of the ground and opened a side pocket, sending the soldiers around us into a panic. Some stepped back while others aggressively moved closer, their weapons aimed in my direction.

Slowly, I slid my hand out of the pocket, holding up at teeny-tiny gold key that had come with the suitcase. I handed it to one of the soldiers. He stood over the case with the key squished between his thumb and finger, almost losing the tininess in his massive hands. Bending down, he fumbled with the lock. I heard the latches snap and watched my overstuffed suitcase burst open. I don't know if it was the force of the bursting or the desert breeze, but as if it had wings, my cute little pink negligee took flight across the courtyard.

Everyone was stunned and far too embarrassed to look at me or retrieve the frilly garment that was now lying in the middle of the yard. Without thinking, I ran to retrieve it, my sudden move causing the soldiers to yell illegible commands, following me with their weapons. With my hands raised above my head, I slowly grabbed the nightgown off of the ground and ever so slowly walked back to my suitcase, where Cyrus stood with his arms raised above his head. I lowered my hand with the nightie to hand it to the soldier, but instead of taking the garment, he jumped to his feet, motioned he was finished inspecting our things, and walked away in a frazzle, leaving Cyrus and I standing all alone in the courtyard.

"You scared an entire army away!" Cyrus laughed.

I climbed on top of my suitcase, trying to force it closed.

"I'm glad you're enjoying yourself, Mr. I Don't Smoke, carrying 20 cartons of cigarettes!"

Cyrus bent down, pushing on the suitcase. "If it wasn't for you and your distraction, they would have taken my cigarettes, and we'd still be at the end of that line!"

We both looked over at the line, which seemed to be frozen in time. Cyrus reacted quickly by grabbing our bags and heading towards the buses.

"You do know cigarettes aren't good for you?" I said, running to catch up with him.

"I'll tell my family. You wait here; I'm going to find us a bus."

I looked around. This was it. We had made it to the border, we were about to cross into Iran, I would finally be with Kayan and all of this would be over. I watched as Cyrus boarded a bus and waved for me to join him. I was so excited, I wanted to run, but didn't dare.

Cyrus stood inside the bus next to the driver, looking in the direction of the other passengers. He held up his hand to stop me. I looked up and saw the entire bus was filled with young armed soldiers—Persian soldiers dressed in dirty, tattered, fresh-from-the-battlefield military fatigues, guns at their sides. They angrily glared at us.

A couple of them jumped to their feet, aiming their weapons. It was a macho move, and it worked. My thoughts went from being elated to "This is how it ends." I didn't even think to ask why. Cyrus directed them to put their guns down. They didn't listen. Cyrus talked faster than I had ever heard him speak, an occasional stutter here and there. I heard my story being told as the guns slowly lowered. I didn't move.

"We're okay," Cyrus whispered.

Two of the soldiers got up and offered us their seats. I sat on the inside by the window, as far away from anyone as I could get on a crowded bus. I felt the tears starting to slide down my cheeks. I had gone from elated to terrified in less than half a minute. I cried for the first time since our adventure had begun. I was supposed to be safe; this was to be my new home. I turned my face towards the window, hiding from everyone.

"Don't worry. They are Persian soldiers returning from fighting at the border of Iraq. I told them you were on your way to be with your husband, who was also a soldier. We're good."

I was numb. Without looking at Cyrus, I nodded and rested my head against the vibrating window.

X

ALLAH'S SOLDIERS

Large gates opened under the heavily guarded bridge in front of us. Our bus's loud diesel engine started up, and we slowly began to roll through the gates and into Iran. We were followed by several other buses and would later find out they were also filled with Persian soldiers returning from battle.

To my disappointment, Iran looked just like the dry deserts of Turkey. Why did I think it would be any different? What was I expecting—the Emerald City?

Suddenly, loud cheering came from the soldiers on the bus. They stomped their feet and yelled in celebration like it was New Year's Eve. They were home! Cheering could be heard from the other buses as well. The bus driver held up several cassette tapes. There was another round of cheering and individuals yelling out which tape they wanted to hear. It was Persian music, of course. I looked around the bus at these young boys. They looked tired and worn out, but were still exuding that male testosterone. They were so young, and I couldn't help but wonder how this experience had changed who they were before they had become soldiers. Was this what it had been like for Kayan when he was returning from the war? Had he taken this route? Did he ride this very bus?

My brain had trouble wrapping itself around the idea of Kayan fighting anyone. He was the kindest, sweetest man, almost void of ego. Yet there he'd been on the phone, telling me that I hadn't heard from him because he had gone to war. I don't believe my mind will ever wrap itself around hearing those words.

It was night now; many had fallen asleep. Cyrus talked through the night to anyone who would engage with him. He loved getting firsthand insight into what was going on in his country. At one point, the buses pulled to the side of the single lane highway and our driver got off.

Cyrus whispered to me, "You can't see it because it's so dark, but there are entire cities out there." He pointed into the pitch blackness of the night. "Iran has mandatory blackouts so that the Iraqi war planes don't fly over and drop their bombs on the cities. The buses are driving without their lights for the same reason. The

Iraqis would love to take out buses full of enemy soldiers."

I looked out into the darkness, taking in what Cyrus had just told me, and then to the faces of all the tired young boys surrounding us. I wondered how many did not get to go back to their families, how many did not make the ride home.

The excited driver jumped back onto the bus, holding up another handful of music cassettes, and again, the soldiers cheered.

Cyrus leaned towards me. "The drivers swap music with each other. It makes the two-day trip a little less boring." Everyone waited with anticipation as the driver popped in the cassette. Loud Persian music played throughout the bus to a happy audience of soldiers. Personally, I longed for silence.

"Too bad they don't have any Stones or Beatles," I suggested to Cyrus.

"They can't. The new Islamic regime has a lot of laws, and music from outside the country, especially Western civilization, has been banned. It's a different country for me, too," Cyrus remarked.

I knew there would be differences being in any foreign country, but the Middle East was proving to be beyond anything I could have imagined. The next day was more of the same. I could feel the tension from the soldiers. Even if my husband was one of them, I represented why they were there to begin with. I represented the cause of all their problems. I was the evil from the

West that their new religious leader, Khomeini, was warning them about.

From the very beginning of my trip, I started journaling about my experiences along the way. Normally I journal to arrive at some kind of insight about life, but this time when I picked up my journal, it was to tell my story, prove that I was here, and document what happened in case I was never to be seen again. Sounds dramatic, but it was the truth. If anything happened, maybe someone would find my journal and give it to Kayan or my family.

"You're always writing in that book. What are you writing about?" Cyrus asked.

"I'm writing about our trip."

"Am I in your book?"

"Of course. You're my guardian angel."

Cyrus sat up proudly. "Really? Will you read it to me?"

How could I say no to my guardian angel? As I started to read to Cyrus, others on the bus leaned in, trying to hear. They so desperately wanted to know who this American woman riding on their bus was. Cyrus translated for them. He was very proud of his role and how I had interpreted him on the page. Soon the entire bus was listening to every word. Cyrus would fill in the details that he felt were important, maybe even adding a few more for drama's sake—not that we needed any more drama. Even the bus driver was calling for Cyrus to speak up. There was a big part of me that, like most journal writers, wanted to keep the stories to myself; these were my personal thoughts and feelings. But to this bus full of soldiers who hung on every word, my words were so much more.

They gathered around, their faces still streaked with dirt from the war. Some were wrapped in bandages or held onto crutches. It was obvious they were mere shells of the youth they had once been, the innocent boy in them snatched away on some battlefield. So, for just a few moments, they escaped into someone else's story—one that had none of the dark realities of their world—and I took on my new role as the entertainment. I had value.

They started to look at me in a different way, not with the contempt they had once shown. They encouraged me to write, even kept the noise to a quiet roar to help me in my writing. I loved the way they filled the bus with laughter at things that were anything but funny at the time. They made me look at things differently as well. I was no longer seen as the evil American. I had gone from the scary unknown that represented everything they hated to being one of them. Even though we came from different backgrounds, we had more in common than not. All of us, myself included, had been affected by the war and the sadness that came with it.

The majority of these boys had signed up for the army out of a deep loyalty to their country. It was what Allah wanted; they were Allah's soldiers.

After visiting with their families, the ones without injuries would be back on another bus headed once again for the Iraqi border. Instead of sitting in classrooms, laughing with their friends and planning their futures, their reality was knowing they very possibly would not have a future beyond the war. Everything that they had previously known in their world had been turned upside down. Death and destruction surrounded them, but on that bus, we laughed, cried, and found a commonality as people.

They also took on a new role as my protectors. When the bus rolled into a stop and I needed to get off, they would surround me, armed with their guns. They followed me every step of the way. If I needed to use the bathroom or get something to drink, I did so with an armed entourage. They took their roles very seriously. I'm sure anyone passing by looked on with curiosity, thinking, *Who is this valuable, well-guarded foreign woman?*

I learned to move slowly so as not to startle them, reminding myself they were young, inexperienced, and handling guns! My modesty had been lost on the train, but I'd never gotten comfortable with the guns, and now, they surrounded me. They were no longer being pointed at me. They were now a warning to anyone who dared to get near me.

As we drove through the different towns and cities, the soldiers would point out where we were with bits of trivia. Occasionally some would get off at a stop to return to their homes. It was bittersweet, wondering what would become of them. Hoping the war would end before they would have to go back out to fight, I gave each one a silent prayer.

On the night before we would arrive in Tehran, our driver pulled over to the side of the road to do the music swap with another bus. The night darkness hid every-thing from our sight, including the other bus. The driver bounced back into his seat, holding up a cassette and pointing to me, then held one finger over his lips, sug-gesting a secret.

"For you!" he said.

The driver popped in the tape and cranked up the sound of the Beach Boys singing, "I wish they all could be California girls!" The bus came alive. It seemed I wasn't the only one who loved and missed American music. Everyone, including the driver, cheered and sang along. The driver looked at me through his large rear-view mirror. I smiled and gave him a thumbs-up. I had always thought he tolerated me at best, so I made sure to stay out of his way. I knew he saw drama when I got on his bus, which was true. But somehow, I had gone from being hated and a threat to being valued and important, even attracting gifts of illegal music.

It was one Beach Boys song after another, all through the night. Thrown in with the mix were a few from the Beatles and the favorite, Queen's "We Will Rock You"—which was exactly what we did, in the darkness of the night. Rolling down some desolate highway, army boots stomping on the floor, vibrating us in our seats, we knew every word, and we rocked!

XI

BATMANGLIJ ALLEY

The next morning, I awoke to an excited rustle on the bus. I looked to Cyrus for an explanation.

"We're in Tehran!" he yelled. Cyrus didn't do excited, so this was a side of him I had never seen before, but it had been years since he had been home.

Others on the bus leaned towards me. "Tehran!"

I looked out the window, taking in the sights of Tehran. It was a very busy city. Lots of cars and buses that seemed to be going in circles. In the middle of the circle was a defaced statue of someone obviously no longer honored. Huge banners hung from the walls on nearby buildings that bore the face of the new leader, Ayatollah Khomeini.

Cyrus and the others looked onto the city like it was their first time seeing it. There were many changes since the coup had taken place. There were pieces of buildings left standing after being bombed or burned out. Left behind were small remembrances of modern storefronts, reminding those who passed by of a different time. Graffiti in every language, denouncing every country, especially the United States, was crudely painted on what was left of the buildings.

Sadness fell over the bus as we looked at what was left of their city. "Wow, they've destroyed everything," Cyrus said sadly.

Cars started honking their horns and waving excitedly at the bus, welcoming the soldiers home. The soldiers leaned out the windows, waving back as the sadness fell away and the excitement of having arrived home took over once again. The bus came to a sudden stop in the middle of the busy street. Everyone began gathering up their belongings and exiting the bus.

Cyrus stood up. "Come on! Let's find your husband!"

"We're in the middle of the street," I answered.

"Yep, you're in Iran now."

I grabbed my things and started to walk down the aisle, the soldiers parting so I could pass. I looked at the boys standing around me. They shyly nodded. Tears began building up, one or two dropping down my cheeks. I quickly wiped them away. I didn't have the words to express to these young men what it meant to have them keeping me safe during one of the most frightening times of my life. By the looks on their faces, they already knew. I hoped their future would not include any more rides on buses going off to war. I hoped that, like myself, they would have lives that were filled with loved ones and endeavors that made a difference.

I stopped next to the driver. This time I wouldn't hurry past him. "Thank you," I said. He shifted uncomfortably in his seat, looking away while nodding his head.

Outside the bus, Cyrus and several other soldiers joined me. "They want to make sure you get to your husband," Cyrus said. They seemed almost as excited as I was to find Kayan.

Cars on the street raced around us. Some were honking and yelling congratulatory comments. I watched while Cyrus and the others tried to wave down a taxi. I think the sight of four armed soldiers, Cyrus, and a foreign woman made the drivers drive past us a little faster! Finally, a taxi pulled up. The car didn't say "taxi" on it, but I learned if it pulls over for you, you get in.

The small, unkempt driver stepped out and quickly opened the doors and the trunk to his very small, soon to be smaller, car. Yes, he was a brave soul. He motioned to the guns the soldiers were carrying around their shoulders and pointed to the trunk of his car. Words of defiance were shared between the driver and this small army. My friends were not about to give up the very things that had been saving their lives. I wanted to step in and end the battle, but who was I to make that decision for these young men? And in all honesty, as much as I hated guns, it was those guns that had protected me these last couple of days.

I watched while this little man repeatedly banged on his car trunk, steadfast and strong, but it only took one look from me to change the dynamics.

One of the soldiers looked at me, gave me a nod, and lowered the rifle off his shoulder, placing it into the trunk. Then, one by one, they all slipped off their weapons and added them to the others. A soldier does not give up his weapon easily. I recognized the gift they had just given me. Cyrus and I sat in the front seat. Cyrus was squished next to the driver, leaving me the window seat to look out onto my new world. Everyone else climbed into the back seat of the car, some sitting in each other's laps. We were quite a sight.

I took a deep breath, trying to release all the fear and uncertainness that I had accumulated along my journey. I told myself I could soon rest, knowing I would be with Kayan, thinking about what that would feel like. I dug one of the letters I had received from Kayan with his home address out of my backpack and handed it to Cyrus.

"This is Kayan's address."

Everyone in the car examined the envelope. There was a difference of opinions as to where 8 Moniriyeh Alley was. In the end, it was only the driver's opinion that mattered. Like a Disney cartoon, we took off in the small, overstuffed car with body parts hanging out of windows.

I was interested in meeting Tehran for the first time. The majority of the women I saw on the streets were wearing black chadors, which had replaced Western wear thanks to the new Islamic regime. Back in the '30s, the chador had been declared illegal by the Shah at the time, who wanted modernization. But the new Islamic regime believed women should be hidden from men's eyes. They were to be modest and covered from head to toe by the large, billowy fabric of the chador, leaving just enough space for the woman's eyes. Even a small strand of exposed hair could be reason for ridicule. It was a bit frightening. Maybe I had seen too many scary movies with figures covered in black robes, but whatever it was, it would be something I'd have to adjust to. I had never thought about how I would fit in, not being a Muslim or Iranian. I hadn't thought dress would matter to me.

A few women were wearing Western clothes, which was a comforting sight. I was looking for ways I could fit into this new world. What would the word "assimilate" look like for me? It seemed the men were given the freedom to dress the way they wanted to; whatever changes had taken place for women did not apply to men. They wore regular attire: jeans, suits, and lots of military outfits.

As we drove through town, every other building or storefront we passed had been bombed out, some for entire blocks.

I looked at Cyrus for answers. "War," Cyrus shook his head.

Cyrus asked the driver questions about what we were seeing. Like a voice in a documentary, the driver narrated, pointing out the history of the destruction in front of us. This included dramatic mannerisms, sadly moving his head from side to side, using hand gestures, looking up to the heavens and clasping his hands in prayer, and tsking. Lots of tsking.

As much as I wanted to hear the stories, I also wished he would keep his hands on the steering wheel! I understood talking with your hands was cultural for Persians. I had learned that from Kayan. I loved teasing him by moving my hands erratically when he was deep in a conversation. He'd respond by grabbing my hands and holding them with only one of his and showing me who was in control.

In Tehran it seemed everyone drove however they wanted with little regard for laws or rules. Our car quickly turned a sharp corner, throwing everyone around in the back seat. We were so tightly jammed in in the front that we barely leaned into one another. Not missing a beat, the driver continued his storytelling.

Cyrus anxiously shared with me what the driver was saying. "He says people burned and looted all the businesses when the Shah was overthrown, especially anything that had connections to America or any other foreign country. They took their anger out anywhere they could. Others just wanted an excuse to steal and be destructive. The sad part is that now people don't have businesses to shop from and the shop owners have lost everything." There was a sad acknowledgement from everyone in the car.

The taxi quickly drove up and down streets and alleys, and after seeing the same flower stand for the third time, I deduced we were lost. The letter from Kayan was passed around in the car, fingers pointing in different directions as we drove by the flower stand again. I had learned a long time ago never to try to tell a man where to go or how to get there. This time there were six of them. All I could say was, "There's the flower stand again."

If I weren't so anxious to get to Kayan, I would have found humor in the situation. We must have looked pretty funny, all crammed into this tiny car going in circles.

And then it happened. The driver pulled over, rolled down his window, and asked a passerby for directions!

Other people on the street gathered and joined in on the conversation. An animated debate ensued with everyone looking at me, each satisfying his or her personal curiosity. The driver nodded with new confidence.

It wasn't easy for me to say and do nothing and allow others, complete strangers, to make choices for my life. This new role didn't fit me well at all.

The driver took off energetically, speaking in Persian to Cyrus. Cyrus quickly interpreted. "He says the name of the street has been changed to your last name, Batmanglij, in honor of your husband's brothers who were killed at war. We were looking for the wrong street!"

The rest of the ride in the car was silent, acknowledging the loss of two young lives and the reality that it could have been any one of these young men having a street named after them. The driver pulled up to a narrow cobblestoned alley. As far as my eyes could see, there were eight-foot-high white and beige plaster walls hiding homes behind them.

The driver yelled to several young boys who were playing in a tall gutter that carried dirty water down the middle of the walkways. The boys cautiously approached the car. I didn't blame them. We were an odd sight, and, if you didn't know any better, a little scary. The driver waved the piece of paper in front of them, pointing to Kayan's address and repeating "Batmanglij" several times. The boys looked over the piece of paper, argued amongst themselves, and then quickly ran off like they were on a scavenger hunt.

"They've gone to get your husband," the driver announced. The words took my breath away. Could this be true? I wanted to run after them.

Cyrus saw my eagerness. "They're kids. Let's make sure we're in the right place."

I looked at Cyrus, hearing him and knowing he was right. Many times Cyrus became the voice of reason. After spending so much time together, he and I had adopted an unspoken language between us. I think it was a side effect of the adrenaline we had been sharing and living with for so long. But it had also became a necessity to know each other's thoughts, especially when it came to making quick, lifesaving decisions. Now, we had naturally fallen into our roles. I was the driven one, my mission clear. I had also come with a sixth sense about things, like my reaction to the woman at the Sheraton. Cyrus now counted on my gut feelings as part of the decision-making process. Although he felt those gut feelings too, he wouldn't allow himself to follow anything that wasn't tangible.

Cyrus had taken on the role of guide and translator. This was his world, and we had become one hell of a team. I don't think either of us thought about the time coming for us to part and what that would feel like.

The kids returned alone and out of breath, yelling at the driver. My heart fell. The reality of actually seeing Kayan had not set in anyway. There had been so much that didn't go as planned that I had lost most expectations.

Then, from down one of the alleys, a group of women dressed in long black chadors, seemingly floating around them, approached and stood in front of us. Before I could say anything, the women parted and standing in the middle of them was Kayan!

Kayan pushed himself through the women, struggling to see into the car. Panicking, I tried to open my door, afraid I would lose him if I didn't move quickly. Kayan reached in and pulled me out. I felt like a child who had strayed from home, now found. He held my face in his hands. Saying nothing, he kissed me.

The women with Kayan were his mother and two of his sisters, 11-year-old Tala and Fariba, who was in her thirties. I stood there while these strangers cried and hugged me through Kayan's embrace. Kayan pulled back and proudly introduced me to his mother while he awkwardly attempted to wipe the tears from his and my face.

Kayan's mother looked nothing like the picture we had on our counter at home. In the picture she looked much younger, was wearing Western clothing, and had Kayan's huge smile. The woman holding me had tufts of gray hair that were struggling to free themselves from under the chador tightly wrapped around her head. There was no sign of that smile. I could feel her sobs from under the black draping garment. It was hard to tell where she began or ended in all that fabric.

By now everyone had gotten out of the car. Kayan pulled me away from his mother. "Where have you been? I've been having people searching everywhere! Your parents have been so worried. We all were," he said in a scolding tone. I could tell he was scared. When Kayan was done saying what he needed to say, I responded calmly, explaining the situation with the plane, but it was information he had already learned from going to the airport to pick me up. He reached out and held me.

I almost forgot about my new friends until I heard their awkward shuffling.

"Kayan, these are my friends."

Cyrus reached his hand out to Kayan. Kayan shook Cyrus's hand, but with a bit of hesitancy that took me aback. How could Kayan do anything but embrace these men and thank them for saving his wife? But he didn't. He looked at Cyrus and the other men in a threatened way. At the time I didn't get it. I felt badly that he wasn't giving these kind saviors the appreciation they deserved. Everyone understood it but me. It was a male thing, a sort of standoff. After all, who were these men showing up with his wife who had been missing for days?

I attempted to fill in some of the blanks for him. He immediately shared them with his family, his mother's disapproving eyes edging out from behind her chador.

"Kayan, this is Cyrus. We met on the plane to Turkey. He's just gotten his degree from the States and is on his way home here in Iran. He had a ticket on the same flight as I did. If it wasn't for him, I don't know if I would have made it. He's my friend, and this is my own army that made sure I made it safely to you!" My army stood proudly in front of Kayan as he greeted them as one of his own. Kayan stepped in front of Cyrus, speaking Persian to him. Whatever was said seemed to unite everyone a bit.

The taxi driver honked his horn. We all looked in his direction, forgetting for a moment he had a job. He honked again. The time had come when everyone had to go their own way, including me. I looked at each face, and even though I was aware of Kayan's jealousy, I hugged each and every one of them, stopping at Cyrus, the tall stranger who never left my side nor I his. If we'd had time, I know we would have lingered a bit more in the moment, sharing the memory of our experience. I know it would have included a laugh or two.

The driver honked again, tapping the horn several times. Cyrus smiled and shrugged his head to one side. I quickly hugged him tightly. "Thank you," I whispered softly in his ear.

Kayan watched, trying to understand our relationship. It would never happen. He would never know that our bond for each other had come as a necessity in order to survive. I had grown to love Cyrus—not just because he had taken it upon himself to make sure I was always safe on our journey, but because he was kind, intelligent, very serious most of the time, but had learned to laugh at almost anything. He was my friend.

I hugged him and wished him a wonderful life. I could see tears starting to accumulate in Cyrus's eyes, something I had not seen before, and with that, he hurried everyone back into the car. I watched while they drove away, honking and waving with their arms out the windows.

XII

TEAL GATES

Iturned and faced Kayan. He looked different than the happy, full-of-energy man I knew. His color was gray, his face thin and drawn, but more than his looks, I felt an emotional disconnect until I remembered what he had just been through. I took his hand, letting him know I was there.

A crowd of neighbors began to gather. Word had spread throughout the neighborhood that the foreign wife of their lifelong neighbor had arrived from America. That seemed to shift the mood. Kayan proudly stood by my side.

"Everyone's been waiting for you," he said. I squeezed Kayan's hand, fighting off the lost feelings. I looked around at all the happy faces welcoming me. I was home.

The neighborhood was not like anything I had ever seen. The blocks of homes were separated by walkways with the same foot-high cement gutter, called a jube, running down the middle. There were no yards or trees, nothing green at all. There were only those eight-foot-high plaster walls, piquing my curiosity about what they were protecting.

Tala, being the 11-year-old that she was, talked all the way to the house in very broken English. She was so excited to have an American sister-in-law to practice her English with. Kayan stopped in front of a large teal-colored metal gate, pointing out the number eight written in Persian. "That's the number eight in case you get lost," he said with authority.

"Lost, Kayan? I've been lost for days in two different countries. I'm not going anywhere without you."

"I know you; you'll be off exploring."

He was right. I wasn't one to sit around. I never wanted to miss anything. I looked at the number eight written in Persian and tried to etch it into my mind. The teal-colored gates showed many years of wear. There were different colored paints showing through the paint chips—so many it was hard to keep track of all the colors. The teal was inviting and not like most of the other gates that were beige and white.

Kayan's mother opened the teal gate, beckoning me to come inside. There was a large courtyard in front of the house. The floor was made up of small white and blue tiles. The home itself was two stories with a deck that wrapped around the top floor. Everything was made from the same plaster-like white material.

"Our room is upstairs," Kayan said and led me to a very narrow—maybe two feet wide at most—spiral staircase. At the top of the stairs was what would be our new home, consisting of two rooms that flowed into one another. One was a dining room with a French-provincial table and a mirrored armoire. The room looked out of place and had few signs of use. The other room was more like a living room with Persian carpets that covered the floor from wall to wall. The carpets were heavy and gave the floor a soft bounce under my feet. Kayan's father sold rugs for a living, and the home reflected his profession. The largest one was mostly burgundy with a geometric pattern outlined in beige and black. Kayan was very proud of his father's profession. He explained that the rugs were made from wool and always hand-made. I bent down, pulling back a corner of the rug.

"You remember," Kayan laughed.

"I do. You said the value is in the number of knots on the back."

Kayan leaned down, showing me the amazing hand-knotted work.

"This is a very good rug. You can feel it in the thickness." We both stood up, feeling the bounce. "Since the war, the United States has put sanctions on Iran. We can't sell to the States anymore."

In the corner of the room sat an older console television that reminded me of the kind we'd had long ago, when I was little. There was no other furniture, no couch or coffee table. Just a bedroll, rolled up against one wall where we would sleep.

"I know it's not fancy, Lara. This is the poorer area of Tehran, but it's only for right now until we get our own place."

Hearing Kayan's words made me feel badly, knowing he was self-conscious about his home. Considering I had no point of reference, he could have told me it was the Beverly Hills of Iran; it made no difference to me.

There were several vases of wilting flowers on the table. Kayan picked one up and held it out to me. "For you. They're a little dead now, but when we brought them to the airport to pick you up, they looked good. Iran is known for its beautiful flowers."

I giggled. "I know. We passed the same flower shop at least three times trying to find our way here. You didn't tell me the name of the street was changed in honor of your brothers."

Kayan looked uncomfortable with the conversation and sadly put the flowers back on the table. "When you weren't at the airport, I thought you had changed your mind about coming."

I held his face in my hands. His cheeks felt thinner than before; even his dimples looked different. "I traveled through two countries by train and bus to be with you."

Kayan started to weep. "I'm so sorry to have put you through this. I'm sorry that this isn't the life we had in the States. I didn't want to go to war. I wanted to come home to you, to us."

Hearing his words was like a trigger for me. I wanted to lash out, to make him feel what I had felt and feared during all those months of not knowing. I had learned that there is no greater or scarier place than in one's imagination.

"I wish you had told me what you were doing, instead of my not knowing if you were alive or dead."

"Would you have really wanted to know, Lara? Would you have wanted to hear that I was going off to fight in the war with my brother?"

I looked at this broken man in front of me, and I didn't know what to say. I didn't know how to make it all go away for both of us.

"I made a choice, and I'm sorry if it was the wrong one, but I didn't want you to be thinking of me in danger."

"I had that job the day you left. I just wanted you to come home," I answered.

"I told you they wouldn't let me out of the country. What was I supposed to do? Watch my baby brother go off to war while I sat around doing nothing? I'm the oldest son. It is my job to protect the family!"

My answer was yes, but I didn't say a word—the second time I had chosen not to say anything and a big first for me in any situation!

"I tried, Lara. There was nothing I could do to change Sergis's mind. They brainwash everyone into fighting. They show children fighting in the war between cartoons! I hate war, and I will never get over seeing my brother killed in front of me!" Kayan smacked his head repeatedly.

I grabbed his hands, kissing them. "We're together, but no more going off to war!" I wiped the tears from his face, leaving stains on his cheeks.

"I can't. The government wouldn't let me anyway; they don't want a family to lose all the men in case they need to help support the family."

How political, I thought, although I was more grateful than annoyed. Then I noticed the framed pictures of Kayan's brothers, Ali and Sergis, with a small candle burning next to them sitting on the dining room table. I picked up one of the pictures, brushing my hand over the face. "Ali?" I asked.

Kayan nodded and picked up the other picture. "This is Sergis. My mom put them here. We don't have to have them in the room with us."

I took the picture of Sergis from Kayan and placed them both back on the table. "Are you okay?" I asked.

Kayan nodded, playfully grabbing me. "I am now. God, I've missed you. When you get over being mad at me, maybe you can forgive me?"

"I don't know. This is one of those things you spend the rest of your life making up for." I laughed.

"Starting right this minute!" Kayan swung me around.

"What I'd really love is a shower. The bus ride was a dusty one. Then I need to call my family."

Kayan lowered me to the floor. "We need to go into the city to the call center for that. I called them when you didn't get off the plane. Your family was really worried, too. I'll show you where the shower is."

I picked up a change of clothing from my suitcase and followed Kayan down the narrow stairs. He stopped in front of a doorway at the bottom. "This is the toilet. You're not going to like it, but I'll build something better, I promise."

He opened the door to a tiny room, so small you could stand in the middle and touch every wall. In the middle of the floor was a hole and a pitcher of water. I looked up at Kayan.

"I promise I'll make it better." He picked up the pitcher. "You use this to clean yourself."

No words would come out of my mouth. The bathroom on the train was much the same, but for me this was so wrong.

Kayan pulled me out of the room. "We can stay at a hotel."

"We can't afford to stay in a hotel, Kayan."

"I know, let me show you the shower. You're going to like it. My father and I built it years ago."

Before I could respond, Kayan whisked me down a narrow staircase that opened up to a large, room-sized shower that was built under the courtyard. The entire shower was made of small, white, gold-speckled tiles. Against one wall was a little window, and I could see people's feet as they passed by in the courtyard.

Kayan backed out of the shower, hoping I would be appeased and forget about the toilet, or lack thereof. I stood under the hot water for what seemed to be an eternity. Just standing there seemed to wash away more than the dirt, the soap erasing days of travel and bringing me back to myself. It was funny how water had the power to do that.

As I stood there, a hand reached around my waist. I knew that hand and turned to face Kayan, with his childlike smile shining through the spray of the water. We stood there, looking into one another's eyes. Was this the same man I loved and married what now seemed like a lifetime ago?

Kayan reached out, his fingers getting tangled in my long, wet hair. He gently leaned in and kissed me, the water running over our lips and into our mouths.

His familiar touch brought me back to the wonderful memories of our lovemaking and how we explored each other's bodies. The fact that neither one of us was an experienced lover made it all the more exciting.

Time had changed nothing.

XIII

INNOCENCE

"Kayan, I've never been on the back of a bike before. Can't we take a taxi?"

Kayan laughed as he stood in front of a small, thin, scooterish motorbike painted in a patchwork of colors.

"Come on, trust me. You know I'm a good driver."

He repeatedly kicked the starter on the bike. Noises came from the machine, none of which sounded promising.

Before I could object or say a word, Kayan pushed a helmet onto my head, revving the sputtering bike, and patted the small piece of seat behind him.

"Where's your helmet?" I asked. Kayan acted like he couldn't hear me, but I knew he probably only had one and wanted to make sure I was protected. He was like that.

We left the courtyard and moved quickly down the narrow alleyways, at times barely missing the gutter that ran down the middle. So, I made my deal with God, which I often do, asking not to let me die in Iran. As soon as I said it, we popped out onto the busy streets of Tehran. It quickly became obvious that no one had ever bothered to make traffic laws! There were no lanes, at least not to the human eye, and people were angry. They didn't just tap the horn; they laid on it, like it was music to their ears. Of course, Kayan's driving fit right in. I grabbed onto him tightly, feeling that his body was half the size of his old self.

A bus pulled up alongside of us. It was decorated with flowers and banners and had crude Persian writing on white bed sheets that hung down the sides. Large pictures of a young man, no older than 16, were plastered on the sides of the bus. People dressed in all black solemnly walked alongside and behind. The followers were all ages. Some carried flowers, dropping them on the ground as they walked. A voice called out from inside the bus, speaking Persian on a loud bullhorn.

Kayan pulled to the side, letting the bus pass, and yelled back at me, "It's a funeral. Because of the war, they have them every day."

I looked at the bus and noticed Kayan had slipped into that space I had seen him go to whenever the war was brought up. Watching the funeral of this young man was a reminder to both of us it was only by the grace of God it wasn't Kayan. I rested my head against Kayan's back and held him a little tighter.

We pulled up in front of a large stone building with long cement steps leading up to the entrance. Kayan announced, "You can call your family from here."

I slid off the scooter a bit shaken from the ride and slowly started up the stairs. Kayan reached out and pulled the forgotten helmet off my head. We laughed.

The phone center was a busy place. For the first time in a long time, I saw people of other nationalities. There were several groups of people from India wearing beautiful silken layers of dress and color. I missed color. As we entered the center, we were immediately approached by security and given the go-over that I was now accustomed to. They searched my purse and asked me to empty my pockets. When they were satisfied with their inspection, we started to walk away. One of the security officers ran up to me, holding out a box. Inside the box were scarfs. He aggressively shook the box in front of me. I looked up at Kayan.

"He wants you to cover your head." Kayan looked uncomfortable with the request.

"Why?" I asked the security officer, who shook the box a little harder.

"The new government is Islamic and women are supposed to cover their heads or wear a chador," Kayan answered.

"But I'm an American and not Islamic. What is the purpose of covering my head?"

Kayan shuffled his feet and looked down at the ground. "Women wear the chador to help men control themselves."

"Well, why don't men cover themselves if they have a problem?"

"I'm sorry, Lara. It's the way things are now. It didn't use to be like this, but this is also a government building."

I looked at the scarfs in the box, picked out the one with the brightest colors, which wasn't saying much, and laid it on top of my head. The security officer sneered with his accomplishment and walked away. At the time we didn't make much of it. All I could think about was making the call to my family.

The phone center looked more like it was Khomeini's headquarters. There were banners and placards placed everywhere. Most were of Khomeini; some were of armed military soldiers being used for recruiting. It was the government's attempt to make fighting in the war the righteous thing to do. There was little else inside the center except several women employees sitting behind counters. They were all wearing what is called a hijab, a scarf tied tightly over their heads and long enough to cover their necks. It was an equivalent to the chador with less fabric, making them easier to work in but serving the same purpose: covering women.

Kayan paid the woman in front of us to make the call.

"I'll have to learn the currency. I don't want to be taken advantage of," I told him.

He looked at me, noting the scarf on my head. "You look cute."

We both smiled, knowing it wasn't true. The woman behind the counter directed us to a corner of the large open room. European-looking phones sat in the middle of several tables. I could tell they had attempted to create a private setting, but they hadn't been very good at it. I paused, thinking of what to say to my family. Kayan rested his hand on my shoulder.

The phone played all the funny sounds and noises that happen when you call overseas. My brother answered the phone. "Hey, Mom! Lara's alive!" he yelled to my mom.

I could hear her struggling to get the phone from Mark. The relief in my mom's voice was the most emotional I had ever heard her; it was a mix of ecstasy and sorrow all wrapped into one sound. I realized I had given her and my family the same experience I had when I didn't know where Kayan was. It was cruel, it was emotionally excruciating. I wished I could take it back. There were sobs on both ends of the phone.

"I'm so sorry, Mom." I wanted to tell her everything that had happened but knew it would only support the fear she was already feeling. "Everything is wonderful, Mom. Kayan is here."

Kayan yelled into the phone, "Hi, Mom, Lara is here with me. Miss you, too." He sniffled, holding back tears as he turned away.

"I promise I'll be safe. Not to worry, Mom. I love you all so much. Tell Dad I love him. Yes, I'll write." I hung up the phone knowing that what I said had been a lie.

Outside the phone center Kayan held me while every ounce of sadness exited my body. I missed my family. I missed their love, and I missed my world. When I thought the sadness had passed, I took a deep breath, pulled the scarf off of my head, and dropped it into the box in front of the security guard.

"Okay, where to?" I asked, taking the helmet from Kayan.

He spoke cautiously. "I know how you love to shop; you're going to love this place," he said, obviously wanting to make things better.

Honestly, I wasn't a shopper. Kayan saw all women as shoppers. A bit sexist, but I recognized his wanting to make me happy, and that always felt good. I hugged him—grateful we were together.

We arrived at a huge open mart that had row after row of tents and tables. There were hundreds of shoppers all wearing the chador, making the market look like a sea of black.

"I've got to park the bike. You wait right here. Don't move, I'll be right back," Kayan said firmly.

I nodded and watched him walk away. My legs wanted to take me exploring. There really was so much to see. One booth had all sorts of copper and gold pots. I realized how spoiled we are in the States with our malls, each individual store representing its multitudes of products, but this was far more exciting. I noticed people, especially women, seemed to be giving me dirty looks as they passed.

I tried not to notice, telling myself I was mistaken and dismissing my thoughts.

"American!" a woman called out in front of me, before spitting at my feet and disappearing into the crowd. Stunned, I looked through the crowd of hundreds. Kayan had long disappeared from my view. The familiar feeling of panic was making its way through my body, and just like all the other times, I didn't understand the whys, what's, or who's, but I knew now was not the time to figure it out.

I looked for my escape. I looked for Kayan, remembering his last words: "Wait right here." My mind went into overdrive. The chadors had created a solid dark wall in front of me. Then from out of nowhere, I was hit in my ribs so hard that I immediately doubled over from the pain.

"I was calling you!" Kayan spun me around to face him, noticing me holding my side. "What's wrong?"

"Someone hit me and another woman spit at me!"

"What, why would someone do that?" he asked, as if I had more information on the assault. Without an answer, I just shook my head. "Come on, Lara, you probably just got in someone's way. Let's go look around."

I wanted to believe what Kayan was saying, that it was just a fluke. Wanting to believe and believing were two different things.

We started to wander in and around the booths. One had rugs piled so high I wondered if a person could survive if they were to fall on top of them. Definitely not OSHA approved. There were several tables displaying sweet-smelling spices with golden turmeric and red saffron in wooden bowls. People were waiting in line for plates piled high with white rice and an array of different kinds of barbecued kabobs that were being handed out. The smells were inviting and teased my nose, all the different scents mixing together.

A woman passed us and yelled something in Persian that ended in "American!" Kayan's shocked and silent stare followed the woman.

"Kayan, what did she say?" I asked.

What Kayan didn't know was I had already experienced racism and was now well aware of its dangers.

"Nothing, she said nothing, stupid old woman."

I knew he was lying, but before I could say anything else, Kayan grabbed me by the arm and led me away. "We should go!" He moved more quickly now, pulling me behind him. I could feel anger from the crowd as we passed. It was no longer just in my head. Things were being said as we passed. Kayan pulled me closer to him.

We found the bike and Kayan hopped on, trying to quickly kick start it. He kicked it over and over, but it only gave back funny noises. I could see a group of women heading our way. They looked more like a lynch mob than shoppers, waving their fists in the air.

"Kayan, hurry!"

Amongst spurts and sputters, the bike started. There was no time to put on my helmet.

"Lara, jump on!" I jumped onto the back of the bike and we took off through the crowd. I don't know how we didn't hit anyone. The bazaar seemed to be endless as we weaved through the booths and people, finally making a turn that took us into an alley. After we rode for some time, Kayan pulled over. We both got off the bike, shaking.

Kayan grabbed and hugged me so tightly that I could feel the soreness of my ribs from the previous assault.

"What the hell was that about? Those women wanted to kill me!" I yelled.

Kayan was still breathing hard, as if he had just finished a race. He bent over and touched his knees. "I have no idea; I've never seen people in my country act that way!"

He grabbed me again and pulled me to him. I could feel his heart beating through his chest. We both just stood there in the silence, taking in our experience but not knowing what to do with it. "I'm sorry. I'm so, so sorry, Lara."

I fought back tears, mostly caused by frustration. I hated when tears decided, all on their own, to show up. *Take a deep breath*, I told myself. I could hear Kayan talking but was unable to climb out of my emotional state to take in his words. "Lara, are you okay?"

Hell no, I wasn't okay. I was tired. I no longer knew who I was and didn't understand how I had become hated by so many! "I'm fine," I answered.

Kayan made the decision that what had happened was an isolated incident and from now on shopping at the bazaar was off our to-do list. I wanted to believe what he was saying about the encounter being isolated. He made a point of taking a more peaceful route home, down side alleys. Within a short time, he was holding his arms out, flapping them like bird wings and getting me to join in.

Kayan always loved teasing. As we rode, he kept moving the bike ever so close to the gutter. He delighted in my screams of fear, and I delighted in his laughter.

XIV

HOME

By the time we got back to the house, we had pushed our experience at the bazaar out of our thoughts. We entered the courtyard with me riding on Kayan's back, laughing like we always had. Kayan's mother and father stood looking at us oddly. It was obvious she had never ridden on her husband's back. I slid down.

"Lara, this is my father."

Kayan's father was noticeably older than his mother. He was short and small in stature. Kayan was tall and well built. He had talked about his father in the past, but in a detached way. There were no childhood stories or memories about the things they did together. All I knew was he sold Persian rugs, as did most of his family. I held my hand out to shake his. He reached out, shook my hand, and smiled the kind of smile one does when they approve of you. I liked him already.

Kayan's mother was different. She was not a person to smile, but considering she had just lost two sons, I couldn't imagine what she felt. Everyone seemed to lower their heads when they saw her. I don't know if it was to avoid the pain she was going through or to avoid her. I found myself doing the same.

Kayan's 13-year-old brother, Ahmed, walked up to me and extended his hand. He had a young presence with just the right amount of cockiness that told you he was a teenager.

"Lara, this is my little brother Ahmed."

The word "little" caused Ahmed to immediately sock Kayan in the arm. He was trying so hard to be mature, and Kayan had brought him to his knees with his words. A wrestling match ensued with Kayan's mother yelling at the two. The little boy had come out in both of them, making them oblivious to anyone else.

Tala immediately moved to my side. She wanted desperately to bond with her new sister-in-law. "Boys," I said. Tala grimaced and looked at me for anti-boy support, which I gladly gave her.

That evening we all shared a traditional Persian meal in the family room downstairs. The only furniture in the room was a square table that sat one foot above a beautiful hunter green and gold carpet. Blankets and a tablecloth were draped over the table with bunches of the extra fabric resting on the floor. A variety of green paisley pillows surrounded it.

"You're going to love this, Lara. Sit down." Kayan sat down at one end and pulled a pillow next to him for me to sit on.

"It's called a korsi. Put your feet underneath." I sat down and put my legs under the table. Underneath was a small heater that warmed your feet and legs. It was heavenly.

The room we were in served many purposes. This was the gathering room for the family. Persian rugs covered the floors, and against the walls were the bedrolls, one for each family member. When night came, this room would become the family bedroom, and no one complained. This was how they'd grown up, and it was accepted. I think in some way it gave them comfort, everyone sleeping within arm's length of each other.

The meal that night consisted of white rice, which Is customary. On top of the rice was a stew of mixed vegetables and meat. It contained a heavy dose of curry with an aroma that permeated the room. Kayan leaned over to speak to me.

"I told my mom what a good cook you are. I also told her about what happened at the bazaar."

"Did you tell her about our being chased?"

Kayan's mother nodded at me, and I smiled back. She didn't understand a word of English and my Persian was minimal at best. Back in the States there was little need for me to learn Persian. But since being on the bus, where it was the only language spoken, I had started to teach myself. Whenever I tried speaking Persian, everyone would smile and laugh, acting as if it was the cutest thing. Definitely not a confidence booster. I didn't want to be cute. I wanted to be listened to and taken seriously. How else would I be able to function in this new world? Fortunately for me, the Shah had English taught in the schools, which helped me to communicate with the younger generation like Ahmed and Tala.

Kayan translated what I had said to his parents and the details of the bazaar experience. His mother and father shook their heads, finding the story difficult to believe or understand.

"See, I told you that was just weird. The people in Iran are nice," Kayan said, sounding relieved.

"But they will always feed you, to make you fat!" Ahmed said, laughing and puffing out his cheeks.

Everyone laughed and continued to share stories with each other, speaking Persian. Although I didn't understand most of what they were saying, I did like watching the family dynamics. Hearing everyone disregard the story about what had happened in the bazaar gave me peace. It was just a fluke.

At night, Kayan and I returned to our room upstairs. It had taken on the role of our sanctuary. It was the one place that we could simply be us. In our room it wasn't Persian Kayan or American Lara. That night, in the dark room, we lay on the floor in our bed, wrapped up in each other, searching for the two people we used to be. It had been a very long time since we had shared that kind of space. I often thought about what our life would have been like if Kayan had never gotten that call from his mother telling him about the death of his brother and asking him to come home. Some people say things show up at your door for a reason. I didn't feel that way. It felt more like a SWAT team had shown up with a battering ram and pushed its way into our lives without even a knock so we could get properly dressed before answering.

There was a lot to try to decipher. Kayan barely spoke about the war or anything that had gone on in the last 11 months. It was obvious he was not ready to revisit the experience. I didn't even know the questions to ask.

Suddenly a loud siren blared, shaking any sense of peace out of me.

"It's okay, we have mandatory blackouts every night at 8:00."

Kayan jumped up and turned off the ceiling light over our heads. The only light left in the room was the softest glow that came from the small candle in front of Kayan's brothers' pictures, a solemn reminder.

"So, Iraq doesn't know where to drop their bombs," I added, sharing the knowledge I had learned on the bus.

Ignoring the reality of my statement, Kayan ran back to our bed. "It's kind of romantic," he said, kissing my neck and shoulders.

I felt anything but romance. I was locked in the thoughts of bombs being dropped. But for Kayan, this was the norm. He had clearly adjusted to his new world. I would need more time.

In the middle of the night, I woke up screaming. I was dreaming that I was being chased on that slow-moving train through Turkey. The train halls were endless. I just ran and ran, looking for a way out. Kayan gently woke me up by brushing the hair away from my face and kissing me on my forehead. I curled up in a ball against him, putting all the mental pieces back together as to where I was and, more importantly, that I was with Kayan before allowing myself to fall back to sleep.

The next morning Kayan woke me holding out a small cardboard box that contained tiny cream puffs dusted with powdered sugar. He sat next to me and guided one towards my mouth. This man knew me well. Tasting the sweet sugary pastry in my mouth made my love of sugar come alive. We both laughed with the powdered sugar adhering to our faces and blankets.

"I got up early and waited in line to get these for my wife. I knew you'd love them."

With a mouth full of sugar, I responded, "You are the best husband in the world!" I kissed him.

"Do you want to talk about your dream?" Kayan asked.

"Not really, just a silly dream," I said, knowing that wasn't the truth.

Like Kayan and his experiences at war, I didn't want to revisit being on the train or any part of my prior journey. What little I did say didn't seem to register with him anyway. At least not the way I had experienced it. He only saw his wife being with other men. It was best to leave it in the past. But the rest of the Batmanglij family wanted to know what had happened that night after hearing my screams. His father jokingly asked Kayan if he was abusing me. It was nice to hear the laughter even if it was at my expense.

After returning from the war, Kayan had gotten a job at a local school teaching English. He was already making plans for me to work with him in the future. I hadn't thought that far ahead, but I liked the idea of having future plans.

"Do you have to go, Kayan? What am I going to do all day?" I was still lying in the bed, with no motivation to do anything else.

Kayan jumped on top of me with distracting kisses. "I have to go to work. Ahmed and Tala will be home around 2:00; they'll keep you busy! Remember Iran has three-day weekends starting Friday, which is tomorrow. Iran is looking pretty good, huh?"

He got up and grabbed a large, folded piece of white fabric that looked like a sheet with little blue flowers on it and handed it to me. "This is for you, if you want to try it."

I examined the fabric. "What is it?" I asked.

Kayan shrugged; it was obvious this was yet another one of those uncomfortable conversations.

"A chador, but it's not black. Black ones are mostly worn by those who are religious or in mourning. My mother got it for you. I love you, Lara Batmanglij." Kayan fled our room to avoid my complaints.

"Whatever. You can keep your three-day weekends!" I threw the cloth at the door.

Wearing a chador went against everything I stood for and Kayan knew it. I saw it as another way for men to control women. I'd grown up in the '60s and '70s, a time when women were encouraged to have a voice and use it. I was grateful for all those women before me who stood up and demanded rights and freedoms for women, freedoms that had been denied before. Was I now willing to go against what I believed in to appease a male religious right? I also knew a piece of cloth would not be enough to keep the secret of who I was. I didn't want to be a secret.

Frustrated, I looked around the room for something to keep me occupied. I picked up my journal and the one book that I could fit in my suitcase. It was a book of affirmations I had taken off my mother's shelf. It was about deciding what you want and affirming it with the idea of bringing it into your life. Problem was, I didn't know what I wanted. I hoped my journal would help me figure that part out.

There was a rooftop above our room accessible by a small flight of narrow steps that Kayan had shown me the day before. I think he wanted my new world to feel bigger than it actually was. I decided the fresh air would be a good place to write. The only things on the roof were jars of vegetables pickling in the sun and a line to dry clothes. Being up there also gave me a better perspective on this new world. All the roofs were a little different; there were no track homes here. The majority of the roofs had laundry hanging or women beating rugs with some kind of stick. Some of the homes had trees growing in their courtyards. I had tree envy. Even when we were in the city, I didn't note much greenery. The trees that were there held a beige dust from all the diesel buses and cars. Everything looked a bit beige from the smog in the air, much like Los Angeles before they added smog devices on cars. I could still remember the stinging in my eyes and residue left on my hair after going downtown as a small child.

When Kayan had showed me the roof, I noticed a young woman on the roof next door. She looked like she was close to my age. As she was hanging out her laundry, she shyly looked at me and I her. I watched as she struggled to put clothes on the line. The oversized chador she was wearing limited her ability to easily move her arms. From her silhouette, I could see she was pregnant. Kayan explained that she and her husband recently moved in. They were the mystery neighbors that no one knew anything about. He said it in a suspicious way.

"Possible Khomeini spies?" I jokingly asked.

"You never know," he replied.

Instead of writing, I basked in the sun and munched on small, pickled onions that were stored in a huge glass jar, lost in thought as to what our everyday lives were going to look like. As it got later in the day, I watched young children playing and a constant flow of women passing by carrying their groceries. Kayan had shown me vouchers given out by the government for food and gas since the war. It was mostly women who would leave early in the morning to acquire the things they needed. He said there were long lines that could take hours to get through, but it had become an accepted way of life by now.

The mystery neighbor appeared on her roof carrying another basket of laundry. We looked at each other and smiled. There was a loneliness about her and probably about me as well. In an odd way, we connected. I wasn't alone anymore. While she attended to her chores, I finally found the words to write. I didn't have an audience like I had on the bus, but the words flowed. It was my way of getting all the thoughts and feelings out, and boy, did they come out!

That day I consciously stayed away from downstairs. It was obvious that Kayan's mother ruled the roost, and I made her nervous. In the morning a woman showed up to clean. She swept and washed the tiled floors with a handmade short broom. At one point she ventured to our room, gesturing to indicate she wanted to clean it. I shook my head no, not wanting or being used to anyone cleaning up after me. Kayan later explained that women in the neighborhood would volunteer to help around the house or do other tasks to help the family after the loss of his brothers. It was customary to do so.

That same day, several women came to visit Kayan's mother, and with a hand gesture she asked me to come join them. I really didn't want to meet anyone. I was tired of having people stare and being unable to communicate, but I did the right thing and walked into the small gathering of women. They all wore black chadors but didn't use them to cover their faces. We shared pleasant nods of acknowledgement and smiles. Kayan's mother brought out a large hookah pipe and set it in the middle of the courtyard. I watched while another woman filled a small metal basket with little pieces of charcoal. The basket had metal chains hanging from it. The woman lit the charcoal and began swinging the basket, causing the charcoal to ignite with sparks and giving it a bright red glow. It took a lot of effort to get charcoal to burn. Then the charcoal was placed in the pipe with the tobacco and the women took their seats on the floor, motioning for me to sit with them. Oh, how I wanted to run away.

Not wanting to insult anyone, I took my seat next to Kayan's mother. She squeezed my hand in an affectionate way. I was glad I had chosen to stay.

The hookah pipe was rather ornate with swirling designs carved into the metal. It stood about three feet tall and had a narrow hose that would deliver the smoke to the person on the other end. One by one, they took a puff from the pipe. Kayan's mother passed it to me and demonstrated how to use it. A part of me wondered what was in the tobacco mixture that made it so important to go to all this trouble. Was it safe? Were they getting high?

I looked around at this group of unassuming women. They were all aged 50 and above. There wasn't an extrovert in the bunch. They had obviously found their tribe. It was no different than a tea party, I told myself. But I had never smoked before, and when the pipe was passed to me, I could feel the peer pressure that I had been warned about as a teenager. I caved, wanting the approval of this group of women, wanting to make a place for myself in my new environment. I reached out and took the pipe.

I coughed, I choked, I gagged, and the women rolled with laughter. One ran to get me a glass of water. I smiled, stood up, and excused myself, hacking all the way to my room. The laughter went on for the rest of their visit. Yes, it was at my expense, but it was a small sacrifice to see this somber group of women enjoying themselves.

I lay down, tasting the foul taste of tobacco in my mouth. There was a knock on my door, and before I could say a word, Tala busted in and joined me on the floor. She seemed so out of place in this country.

"Hello, Lara!" Tala was clear and calculating in her words. Ahh, English words. They sounded so good.

"Hello, Tala, how are you?"

Tala repeated my words over and over. "Teach me more!"

We shared words back and forth. Tala wanted each word to sound so perfect that they all came out of her mouth stiff like cardboard.

I liked Tala. She had a great energy; everything excited her, and I mean everything. It was hard to keep up with her quick thinking. But it was a challenge I accepted and enjoyed. She looked and acted like the stereotypical almost-teenager. She had long, wavy, never-been-cut black hair, the beginnings of acne on her cheeks, and a personality that went from savvy to schoolgirl in half a second. Of course, we bonded immediately. Mostly I think I enjoyed the way she worshipped me. Tala was stuck in many worlds and wanted to be a grownup. She wanted the boys in the household to live somewhere else, and most of all, she wanted to be a free thinker. The new Iran squelched anything like that from happening. She lived in a male-dominated society where women were second class at best. She was forced to wear a chador, which she hated.

When she looked at me, her eyes lit up at the potential to be more. I couldn't help but tell her all the truths that she was being denied, like that she could do and be anything she wanted. I reminded her how brilliant she was and to not let anyone tell her anything different. She hung on every word because, despite what her present world was telling her, she knew it was true.

There was another knock at my door and Ahmed popped his head in, staring Tala down.

"Tala, go!" Ahmed motioned for Tala to leave.

"Ahmed, you go!" Tala spoke quickly and angrily in Persian.

It was obvious there was sibling rivalry. It was obvious Ahmed liked his role as the family male dominator, even if he only had his little sister to rule over. Tala stood up and faced her brother. Words with dramatic hand gestures flew around the room. It was a dance they had had many times before.

"Ahmed, Tala is fine. She doesn't need to go. I like the company."

I didn't know if he understood my words, but he understood when I reached out and put my arm around Tala. I didn't like the way he spoke or tried to control her. In my world, only a small person did that—and he deserved better, too. He looked at me and lowered his eyes. A woman had put him in his place. I reminded myself there was a child inside of him as well. It may have been chased away by war and the loss of his two brothers, but it was there. I put my arm around him and his wounded ego. Ahmed reached into his pocket and pulled out a white piece of paper. On one side something was written in Persian; the other side was in English.

"For you, they drop from there." Ahmed pointed up and made a plane out of his hands. "True, Lara?"

I read the flyer and was shocked by its content. I read it again. Ahmed and Tala waited for my response. I looked at the two children in front of me.

"No, it's not true. None of this is true. This is called propaganda."

Tala slowly repeated the word "propaganda." The flyer said that a Persian family of six had been visiting the city of San Diego in the United States and had been hung because they were Persian. The flyer gave a detailed description of the family and their children swinging from ropes that would frighten anyone.

I remembered years ago Kayan had told me about the propaganda that was spread throughout Iran during his childhood. Most of it came from their neighbor Russia, and since the people of Iran had little connection to the outside world, who was to say it wasn't true? Kayan had grown up being told that all black people were thieves and murderers. When he first landed at LaGuardia airport in New York, he saw lots of people of color and various nationalities. He was so afraid, he didn't leave the airport until he could get onto his connecting flight. We laughed at the absurdity of the thinking and even harder when I reminded Kayan that when we met, he was attending an almost all black college, living in a mostly black neighborhood, and one of his closest friends was a black male transvestite! I crumpled up the flyer, knowing the damage a simple piece of paper could cause, and wondered how many people had read it and believed it to be true.

Iran was not a melting pot like the United States by any means. The vast majority of the population was Persian and Muslim. On our trip through the city to the phone center, Kayan had pulled over to the side of the road and pointed out a Christian church. At the time I wondered why since I did not attend a church in the States, but for some reason he thought my seeing a church would make me feel more at home.

Kayan busted through the door with the excitement of a five-year-old. "Happy Nowruz!" He was carrying a fishbowl with a goldfish swimming in it and a pie pan with the greenest grass growing. "We have a pet!" he announced.

I ran over and took the fishbowl from Kayan. "Ahh, he's so cute!"

"Hey, what about me?" Kayan complained.

The out-of-place dining room table now had a purpose. I placed the fishbowl in the center and jumped into Kayan's arms. He swung me around in the air, my feet not touching the ground. Tala and Ahmed bolted out of the room, obviously uncomfortable with open affection.

"Lara, you taste like smoke."

Still in Kayan's arms, I nodded yes. "I was smoking with your mom."

He let me drop to the ground. "What?"

"Some of your mom's friends came over, and we had a smoking party. I'm going to learn how to swing the charcoal next time!" I loved teasing him. I could see him stumbling for words.

"I hate when my mom smokes. She only started after my brothers were killed. Lara, we don't smoke!"

Kayan stopped himself short from making the demand that I never smoke again. He knew I was not told what to do, or what not to do. I could see the smoke coming from the brakes he knew to put on. I also decided to let him off the hook.

"Don't worry, Kay. I wasn't very good at it. If they invite me again, I know it will be for entertainment purposes only."

We both laughed and turned our attention to the table with the fish.

"This brings back wonderful memories," I said with a bit of sadness, remembering when Kayan had taken me to my first Nowruz celebration at the college. That was also the first night we made love. The feelings of the memory swept over me.

Kayan leaned his head over my shoulder. "I remember…"

The new regime wanted to ban Nowruz all together. It was not a religious holiday and was pre-Islamic, but the people wouldn't have it. They had grown up with and loved their Nowruz, which begins on the first day of spring and lasts for several weeks.

"Happy Nowruz. Remember, if we can keep the fish alive for a year, we will have a year of good luck. Please try not to kill it!"

"It's a she," I answered.

"Well, there's a fifty-fifty chance you're right."

"She must have a name. Hope, let's call her Hope!" I moved the bowl to a more secure spot on the table.

"Hope it is." Kayan kissed me and held me close to him, my happy place.

"Come on, we're going to the movies!" he shouted.

"Really?" A normal activity sounded wonderful.

"Don't get too excited. Our movies are not like the movies in the States. They're usually musicals from India. I want to invite Tala and Ahmed to go with us. They need to have some fun."

As we started to head out the door, I ran back and reluctantly grabbed my black hooded sweatshirt out of my backpack. I was reluctant because of what it represented to me. Kayan watched silently as I pushed my long blonde hair into its hood. He put his arm around my shoulder as we exited the room.

The four of us walked down the alley towards the city streets. Tala always wore the black chador when she left the house. But as soon as she got home, she would take it off immediately, letting it drop to the floor and allowing the child inside her out.

We took a taxi to the movie theatre. The theatre was large and beautifully decorated with vintage paintings on the walls and ceilings. It was similar to a theatre in Hollywood called Grauman's Chinese Theatre that, at one time, was filled with celebrities at the grand opening of movies.

Inside, the theatre was packed, and it seemed that everyone was also a smoker by the amount of thick gray fog that lingered in front of the screen. It had been years since the States allowed smoking in a theatre. Definitely not in my lifetime. When we walked down the center aisle, the loud chatter subsided as we passed. It was a first for Tala and Ahmed, seeing people's reaction to me. Tala reached around and grabbed onto the other side of Kayan. While Kayan looked for four seats together, I walked with my head down. I wanted to look up and see the faces in the room and try to get an idea of how people were reacting to me in case we needed to leave quickly, the freshness of the bazaar experience still branded in my memory. A kind gentleman stood up and moved his seat, making way for us to sit together.

I don't remember much of the movie. Yes, it was made in India, the actors were Indian, the sets depicted India, and the language was Hindi with Persian subtitles. I was out of luck on all ends. The movie was a musical with high-pitched voices that took some getting used to. I never got used to it. Tala and Ahmed were enthralled by what they were seeing on the screen. I loved watching Kayan enjoying the movie, holding his hand and brushing the soft hair on his arm. He would catch me looking at him and smile that familiar smile. So much I had taken for granted before.

At the same time, I was being cautious by making mental notes as to where the exits were and surveying the people sitting around us. I didn't feel paranoid, even if the bazaar experience was a fluke. As soon as the movie was over, we quickly left the theatre, everyone around us slowly pushing their way out onto the streets.

"Let's get something to eat!" Kayan announced.

Tala excitedly jumped up and down. "Oh yes!"

"Tala!" Ahmed scolded.

He was embarrassed by Tala's show of emotion—not a good quality in a young woman in Iran—and wanted to squash every bit of it. I put my arm around Tala, approving of her behavior. Kayan put his arm around

Ahmed, speaking in Persian to him. Whatever he said made Ahmed smile. It was interesting to watch Kayan in his role as a big brother. He was a good big brother, and I would have expected nothing less.

On almost every street there were people roasting beets placed on the ground in little self-made barbecues resembling a hibachi.

"You have to try this, Lara." Kayan handed the man a few bills and the man gave him a roasted cut-up beet, wrapped in foil. Kayan held up a piece for me to taste. "You love sweet things, try it."

It was delicious, like nothing I had ever tried before. I noticed that the money in Kayan's hand had the Shah's picture on it and had been defaced by turning the Shah's picture into the devil with horns and a pointed beard. I took the bill and examined it.

"They haven't made new currency yet; everyone hates the Shah," Kayan explained.

We continued to walk down the streets, the darkness seeming to hide who I was, giving me solace.

"What about you, Kayan? What do you feel?" I asked.

"Honestly, I try not to feel. I've lost two brothers, almost my own life, and almost you. They say I'm supposed to support this guy Khomeini, who makes decisions from religion, which I don't necessarily believe. No one asked me before and no one asks me now, except for you."

Kayan pulled me in close to him. "What about you? Would you have fallen in love with me if we had met after you saw all this?" He waved his arms, pointing out the burned-out buildings, murals of Khomeini, and graffiti in every language. "Or would you have run away?"

Tala and Ahmed walked ahead, pushing each other with each step, trying to determine the leader of the pack. I stopped and looked at Kayan.

"I didn't fall in love with a country. I fell in love with and do love the beautiful man you are. That didn't change because of war or any of this."

At that moment we happened to look up and noticed a dummy depicting Uncle Sam hanging from a light pole. A breeze caused it to sway ever so slowly. We looked at each other and broke out into laughter. Maybe it was nerves, maybe frustration, or maybe just the absurdity of the moment, but laughter was what came out.

There weren't very many small businesses left in Tehran, but Kayan managed to find a restaurant within walking distance. When the four of us entered, the sounds of people enjoying their meals and conversations slowed. All eyes turned to us, which I was getting used to. A young waiter with a white apron tied smartly around his waist flew across the restaurant and quickly led us from the front room with white tablecloths and flowers on the tables to another much smaller room tucked away in the back. There was no finery in this room.

"Kayan, can we sit in that room? There are plenty of empty tables."

Kayan looked at the waiter, obviously embarrassed to ask the question. He had information I did not. The waiter shrugged and pulled out a chair for me to sit down. I waited for Kayan's response.

Kayan whispered, "We can't sit in that room; it is for men only. This room is for women and families. I'm sorry."

I was stunned. I didn't know whether I should be angry or cry. I had never been treated like I was inferior because I was a woman, or for any reason.

"This is good, Lara," Tala added and immediately sat at the table that was in front of us. Tala had learned at an early age to accept what was given to her. It was obvious that she was a representation of the majority of women in Iran.

Ahmed sat down, insensitive to the moment. I looked back at the room of all men, pleased with their place in life, and then to the small room of women hiding behind chadors, some of them young children. I took my place and sat down. Not much was said between Kayan and me that night.

When we arrived back home, we could hear fireworks from our room, a Nowruz celebration. Kayan flew to the deck to watch them. He begged me to watch with him, but I just didn't have a celebration in me. I was angry and I was hurt. For whatever reason, I blamed Kayan, as if he had the power to change the injustices in his country, or as if I could change the injustices in the United States—and I knew there were plenty. Looking back, I wish I had gone out on that deck and watched the fireworks that were so important to Kayan. I wish I had gone out and oohed and aahed at every one. I wish I had seen their reflection in his eyes and felt his arms around me. But I didn't. I stayed curled up in our bed on the floor, fighting back tears and anger with each breath.

"Lara, we'll be fine. The bazaar was just a bunch of angry old ladies," Kayan whispered in my ear, wrapping his arm around my neck. "You can't live hiding out in the house forever. You have to let it go."

Before I knew it, I was on the back of the bike with Kayan. I tucked my long hair up into the helmet and flipped the visor over my face. The city streets were wall-to-wall buildings except for the daylight that came from those that had been bombed out during the coup. Most of the destruction had happened during the revolution and had nothing to do with the war with Iraq. Since Kayan had still been in the States during the coup, he was shocked when he saw what had been left behind. He had fond memories of Tehran—the businesses they would frequent and the open patios where both men and women would enjoy a meal together. It was hard to imagine looking at it now, but Kayan described the old Tehran in such a way that I could almost see the pleasantries of the people living their daily lives. Now hateful graffiti was painted on everything that was left standing and the smell of diesel filled your lungs with each breath, especially when you were on the back of a motorcycle.

We crossed paths with two funerals that were much like the one from the day before. Mourners walked alongside buses and cars, handing out flowers, while a booming voice could be heard calling out from a bullhorn. I looked at the pictures of the young men that were plastered on the buses and wondered what the man on the bullhorn was saying about them. Maybe he was saying kind words about who they were or what they had done in their short lives. As I watched the pictures of these young men pass, one of the mourners slipped a beautiful white rose into my hand. I looked at the rose, feeling the sadness and loss it represented, and laid my head against Kayan's back, knowing it could have been his picture on a bus.

According to most of the graffiti in the city, the United States and many other countries were responsible for the war and loss of their loved ones, which may have explained people's reactions when they saw me. Maybe I was representing all the bad in their lives. Maybe I was the one person they could take all their anger and pain out on.

If that was the case, the situation for me in Iran could be much worse than Kayan or I could have ever thought.

We pulled up in front of a 10-foot-tall brick wall with iron gates. I immediately recognized it was the American Embassy. There was a feeling of familiarity and a realness that I had not felt from the nightly visits on TV.

"You said you wanted to see the embassy. Not much to see," Kayan yelled over the loud motor on the bike.

He tapped my leg, suggesting I get off so he could park the bike. As I stood in front of the gates, there was a stillness. There were no more demonstrators or crowds of reporters. The building looked abandoned. Tall weeds covered the inside courtyard. A hand-painted sign on the gate read "DEN OF SPIES," denouncing other countries and accusing them of the downfall in Iran. Painted on the top of the building itself, a message in large letters read, "DEATH To AMERICA. VIETNAM WOUNDED YOU, IRAN WILL BURY YOU!"

I reached out and touched the walls, the same walls that had held the hostages for 444 days. It felt surreal. I took the rose that was still in my hand and placed it on the steps that led up to the gates. Sadly, any political point the rebels may have had had been lost throughout the world the minute they entered the sanctity of another country's embassy. But they got the attention they wanted. All eyes were on them and this new regime.

Without thinking, I removed my helmet and took a picture of Kayan and me in front of the historical gates. Immediately, two soldiers from inside the embassy came running towards us with their guns drawn. Kayan grabbed me, pulling me to him and raising his hands above his head. Shocked, I raised mine, too. There was a heated argument in Persian between Kayan and the soldiers. Terrified thoughts of our being taken into the embassy ran through my head. Kayan looked at me and took my camera, handing it to one of the soldiers. We watched while he opened up the back, exposed the film, and handed it back to Kayan. With our hands still in the air, we stood there while the two soldiers walked back and entered the embassy.

It was a quiet ride home. For two days after that I did not leave the house. Kayan would go off to work, and I found myself in a kind of bubble, not wanting to leave the safety of its space.

XV

THE BATTLEFIELD

Tala and Ahmed always rushed home after school. They were excited to share their day with me and practice their English.

"Why don't you watch television?" Ahmed asked.

The older console television sat quietly in the room. I had never thought of turning it on. Ahmed waited for my answer. I had none. Tala shook her head no.

"Tala doesn't like it," Ahmed smiled.

I looked at Tala, waiting for an explanation. She shrugged. Ahmed turned on the television. There was only one channel, and it was controlled by the government.

I threw some pillows on the floor for everyone to sit and enjoy the cartoons currently on the screen. You didn't need translation for cartoons. Sitting on the floor laughing with young people felt so innocent.

The show was interrupted by a special news report. Ahmed delighted in interpreting what we were seeing, which was the recruitment of people, young and old, male and female, going off to war. Children were shown dressed in military fatigues, being taught how to shoot rifles, jump in ditches, and crawl on their bellies. Tala turned away. Now I understood why she didn't like the television.

"Tala doesn't like seeing anything about war, but I do!" Ahmed jumped up and pretended to be shooting a gun.

I looked at Tala and saw that the normally high energy, innocent child had emotionally left the room. What was left was a child sitting on the floor, rocking away her fear. I moved close to her. "It's okay, Tala," I said, consoling her, but it wasn't okay. Tala looked at the pictures of her brothers Ali and Sergis sitting on the table and started to cry.

"War is bad. I miss my brothers. Ahmed wants to go to war too."

I looked at Ahmed, whose attention was locked on the television. What we were watching turned out to be a commercial mixed in with the cartoons. They were recruiting children and older people to join the army. Now I knew why Kayan's brother Sergis had insisted on going to war. They had a way of making war look so exciting and resembling nothing of real life.

Ahmed nodded his head. "They don't let me go. I have to take care of my family, ugh."

Ahmed played soldier, aiming his imaginary gun at Tala. Tala jumped up and started swinging her fists at Ahmed. Tears flowed down her face. Ahmed cheered and welcomed the blows.

I stepped in between them. "Stop!"

The door opened and Kayan entered, quickly pulling Tala away. Ahmed continued to cheer Tala on. Kayan punched Ahmed in the arm, hard enough to cause him to stop and rub away the pain. Tala ran out of the room. I looked at Kayan, not knowing what to say.

"Look!" Ahmed pointed to the television.

On the screen were old men lining up to go off to war. Some were barely able to walk. Many of them were disabled in one way or another, but they were anxiously waiting to get in line.

Ahmed laughed. "We should take Dad!"

"Ahmed!" Kayan continued to scold Ahmed in Persian.

"What is going on, Kayan?" I asked, watching the television screen.

Kayan looked at the screen. "Khomeini tells the old men that no matter what they've done in their lives, if they die fighting for Mohammed, they will go straight to heaven. It's crazy."

We watched as a group of old men dressed in all white outfits began walking across endless dirt minefields. They prayed to Allah with each slow step.

"They are crossing minefields, making them safe for the tanks. They wear white for their trip to heaven," Kayan explained. He looked at my horrified stare. "Okay, that's enough of that."

But my eyes were glued to the horrific scenes being played out on the screen. Excited children, looking no older than eight or nine years old, were dressed as soldiers and wearing red headbands with the words "Sar Allah" written on them. They held up rifles and had little metal keys on chains that hung around their necks.

"Those are children!" I stepped closer to the television, making sure my eyes were seeing correctly.

"Lara, you really don't want to know."

I stared at Kayan, determined to get my answer.

"'Sar Allah' means warriors of God; Khomeini declared that the key was their ticket to paradise," he explained.

"I'm older than them. Why can't I go?" Ahmed demanded.

Without a thought, I socked Ahmed in the arm!

"Oww!"

Kayan switched off the television. Ahmed rubbed his arm and moaned and complained as he walked out of the room.

"That's horrible, Kayan."

Kayan pulled me into his chest "I know. There's worse than that; trust me, I've seen it."

I looked up at him. I wanted to ask him questions but was also afraid of what I would hear. Whatever he had seen or experienced had altered who he was in the process. I could see a glimmer of the sweet, innocent man I had married. He was struggling inside, missing the person he was and trying to weaken the memories from the war.

That evening a young woman showed up at the house. She was Kayan's brother Sergis's girlfriend. Kayan excused himself and went down to meet her in the courtyard. I watched from the window while he spoke to the woman and accepted a small envelope from her. She seemed strong, holding it together, taking deep breaths while she spoke to Kayan. More than once Kayan wiped a tear from the corner of his eye. They were both trying so hard to erect walls around the hurt, trying to keep the pain from getting out, trying to hold it together for the other. They were good. I didn't think I could have done it. I looked at this young woman, knowing that could have been me, wondering why Kayan had been spared when two of his brothers had not.

Kayan graciously walked the young woman to the front gate and showed her out. It was an intimate moment, both of them feeling the loss of someone they loved very much. But there was no physical interaction. This was his brother's girlfriend, a respected relationship.

By the time he returned to the room, he had put together a smile for my sake. He reached out and held me. In many ways this was to be my new role. I was his touchstone, reminding him that he was okay and that there was still light in his world.

Kayan held the envelope in his hand. "Sergis's girlfriend wanted us to have pictures she had taken of him."

It was obvious Kayan was having difficulty looking at the envelope's contents. "Can I see them?" I asked.

Without saying a word, he handed me the envelope. I spread the pictures out on the dining room table and experienced who Sergis was. In the pictures he was funny, silly in some of them, a bit of a flirt in others, and he obviously loved his girlfriend. Some of the pictures were of the couple. With her he stood a little taller, looking a bit more mature, seemingly trying to impress the girl he loved. The last picture was of him in his military uniform. Both Kayan and I cried; we cried not just for the loss of Sergis, but also for the lives these two would not share together.

Kayan spent the rest of the evening sharing the events of the war as he had experienced them. About how he was afraid of getting close to any of his fellow soldiers after seeing so many die next to him. Kayan was not made for a battlefield. He took his place in a war because of his brother. In some imaginary way, he believed he could protect him. He shouldered a terrible guilt for not being able to do so. Kayan had experienced every ugly thing that happens with war. He saw much younger men than himself put on a uniform, barely able to fill it out, proudly march out onto a battlefield, and then be carried home wrapped in a white sheet.

I was processing everything he was saying, not sure what I was supposed to do with my feelings about the awful, unthinkable events. I was still angry about his secretly going off to war and not telling me. Hell, I was angry he went to Iran in the first place!

"Lara, I have to tell you something." I looked up at Kayan. Tears were flowing down his face. "I can't get over that dream I told you about, the one I had the night before Sergis was killed. He laughed when I told him that I dreamt he was going to be killed! I told him, I told him, but he wouldn't listen!"

Kayan fell into a heap on the floor. There was no way I could ever truly understand or feel the pain he was going through. He was different, and I was just beginning to understand why.

SATAN HAS BLUE EYES

In the days that followed, I found myself feeling caged in. I wanted to go out, but after the last experience I chose not to. After Kayan told his family about what had taken place at the bazaar, his mother insisted we were mistaken and took it upon herself to prove her point. One day when Kayan had gone off to work, I was still lying in bed, contemplating this new life and what to do next, when his mother knocked and entered with three other women: Kayan's aunt and two of her friends. They lived in the country and had traveled hours to meet Kayan's wife.

They quickly sat down on the floor around me. Instead of a meet and greet, it felt more like an exorcism. Four strange women circling me, dressed in long black chadors, speaking in a foreign language and staring. None of them spoke any English. Tala and Ahmed, my interpreters, had already gone off to school.

Suddenly, the aunt stood up and motioned for me to follow them. Other than Kayan's mother, they seemed like a pleasant group. They smiled as they beckoned me to leave the house with them. Boy, did it feel good to be on the other side of those gates. The women flanked me on all sides, talking amongst themselves. It felt like a girls' day out. It felt good. Except for the language barrier, it felt normal.

We walked down one street that had little shops lining both sides. A dead lamb hung in front of a meat market, blood covering its white fur. I shivered when I saw it, not knowing how to react. The aunt noticed my reaction and laughed; I could tell she was a happy person. I walked as far as I could around the lamb. I could hear them giggling.

Another group of women passed us and shouted out in Persian, glaring in my direction. The women I was with were surprised by whatever was said and moved closer to me. Another woman passing us spat at the ground in front of me. Kayan's aunt angrily shouted at the woman. I pulled at her arm, not wanting her to fight a battle that obviously had no end. The aunt looked at me. Reaching up, she pulled my face close to her. Staring into her eyes, I could feel her compassion and sorrow for what she was witnessing. Several others passed us and called out, chanting in Persian.

Out of nowhere Kayan appeared, spoke angrily to his mother, and pulled me to him. His mother began to cry and wail. All the while the chanting from women passing by increased.

"Kayan, what are they saying?" I asked.

"They say nothing. They are mean, angry, ugly people!"

"But what are they saying? I need to know."

Kayan paused and looked into my eyes. "They say Satan has blue eyes. It's foolishness, an old belief."

"They think I'm Satan?" I mumbled.

Kayan paused, looking at me. I could still hear the voices of those around us in the background, but Kayan's voice seemed to drown out all the others.

"You are the kindest, most loving person I have ever known. They are looking for someone to take all their anger and pain out on. My mother and aunt should not have brought you here."

"I can't stay locked up in that room forever. There is nothing wrong with who I am. I am not Satan!"

A small group of women started approaching us. Kayan pulled me close to him as we quickly moved away.

Panicked, we all rushed down the streets and alleyways until we came face to face with those large metal teal gates with the number eight written on them. Oh, how I didn't want to go back through those gates. *Satan has blue eyes*. The words kept running through my mind. I stood looking at the teal gates, knowing what I would lose once I crossed through them. Kayan held his hand out, taking me inside.

Once inside, Kayan's aunt hugged me for the longest time. It felt like she was trying to apologize for the unkindness of others. But at that moment, I just wanted to run away. I didn't want anyone's compassion or understanding. I needed my freedom and safety in a world that didn't see me as some sort of evil. The threat of not ever having a normal life in Iran was becoming a reality.

XVII

THE PLAN

That night, Kayan and I lay in bed and talked. For hours we cried, we laughed, and we remembered who we were before all this, cherishing the simplest of memories.

"Kayan, I want you to come home with me," I said.

And there it was, the truth; we both knew there was no life for us if we stayed in Iran. And like an elephant in the room, the truth pulled up a chair and sat with us.

"I want to go home, too, but you know the government won't let me out of the country, Lara. I'm so sorry I got you into this."

I sat up, looking into Kayan's face. "You had no idea how people would react to me."

"I'm just so sorry, Lara."

"You're not responsible for how people from your country are, just as I am not responsible for how people reacted to you in the States after the hostages were taken. Now what are we going to do?"

Kayan cleared his throat. "Some people are illegally crossing the border into Turkey, but there are risks."

"Like?" I was hanging on his every word.

"Like getting caught! In Iran we would be considered traitors and most likely put in jail. But if we get across the border, our papers from the United States should get us safely home, if we are not caught crossing the border."

I knew all too well the dangers of Turkey, and it was the last place I wanted to head for, but that unknown was better than sitting and waiting for something to happen here. Being proactive felt good. *Home.* Kayan had said it. We would both be safe and free to live our lives peacefully, together. We were going home. Those were the only words that mattered to me.

We started laying out our plan to leave Iran. We were excited! Part of our plan was telling Kayan's family that we would be leaving. That night, while we all sat around the korsi sharing our meal, Kayan told his family about our plan.

The conversation was in Persian. We assumed after everyone had witnessed the response to me, they would be supportive. Kayan's mother got to her feet and wailed as if she had received a death sentence. She paced, beat her fists against her heart, and cried. Like a stubborn child, Kayan refused to react to his mother's behavior. He stood strong.

Although I could not understand the language, I could tell the results of what was being said. Kayan grabbed my hand from under the korsi. And then, in an instant, I saw Kayan devastated by whatever his mother had just said to him. Tala and Ahmed jumped to their feet, yelling at their mother, obviously horrified by her words.

"No, Ma, na!" Tala screamed as her mother's cries became more dramatic with each breath.

Kayan's body had shrunk under whatever his mother had said. I could tell he was fighting back tears, but they came anyway, rolling down his cheeks. My normally strong husband was becoming unrecognizable. What words could do this to a human being?

He ignored my attempts to find out what was said.

I looked to Tala, my female confidant.

"My mother said it was Kayan's fault my brother Sergis was killed."

I gasped. Kayan lowered his head into his hands.

I looked at this woman with such disdain. She was so desperate to hold on to her son for her own selfishness that she would say the most hurtful thing she could and didn't care that her cruel words would live on for a lifetime. She turned away from me.

Kayan cried, repeating the words over and over again, "My mother blames me for my brother's death. She said I should have saved him!"

The room became a tornado of angry emotion, everyone yelling. Kayan's mother repeated her words and I pulled Kayan's face towards mine, reminding him of the truth: that he was never responsible for anything his brother did or did not do.

Amidst it all, Kayan's father stood up and yelled something in Persian in a deep, dark tone that shocked everyone. Up until that moment the man had barely spoken at all, but I was grateful he found the strength to stand up for his son and face his wife.

His wife went silent. She looked around, then picked up right where she left off. Frustrated, Kayan's father angrily left the room. Although I did not know what he said, it was obvious he was not known for outbursts. But when all was said and done, he was powerless over his wife.

I stood up and took what was left of Kayan by the hand. I led him away from his mother and into the sanctity of our room. Sadly, all my words could not change the power of what had been said by his mother. Exhausted, we fell asleep still dressed in our clothes.

I was shaken awake by Tala. "Lara, you must come, you must come. Kayan, he has a gun; he's going to kill himself!"

Before I could take in the meaning of her words, I had flown down the stairs. Standing in the doorway of the bedroom, I could see Kayan tearing at the walls with a hammer. Within arm's reach, a large handgun sat on top of the korsi. The whole family was screaming. His father pleaded with Kayan to stop, but Kayan had no reaction to anyone. He was fixated on destroying the wall. Blow after blow, with all his strength, he thrust the hammer into the walls. His black hair was covered in white dust from the plaster. Remnants of the wall were everywhere. Exposed behind the layer of plaster was a wall of clay and dirt. The family stood behind Kayan, crying and screaming—all except for his mother, who stood quietly in the doorway watching, strong and righteous.

I rushed over to him. "It's okay, Kayan, it's okay." I motioned for Ahmed to take the gun.

"It's not okay, everything is my fault. My mom was right, it's my fault that my brother is dead. I should have done something to save him!" Kayan stopped tearing at the wall and looked at me. "What have I done to us?"

I pulled Kayan to his feet. He fell into my arms and whispered in my ear, "I can't stay here, I can't stay in this house!"

As we headed for the door, Kayan's mother whined in Persian. Kayan yelled back at her. We walked out into the night through the teal metal gates; it felt more like walking out of prison. The alley was pitch dark. There weren't streetlights or anything else to light the way, but Kayan seemed to know every step we had to take. We didn't speak; we held tightly onto each other's hands, acknowledging each other's presence.

There was anger in Kayan's steps. I had seen him go from devastating pain to fiery anger within minutes, and I must say, I liked the anger better. I understood the anger because I felt it too. How could a mother say those awful things to her own child? How could this little woman have so much power over Kayan, over us? I couldn't understand why she wouldn't bless his leaving, knowing he would be safe and not marching out onto a battlefield like her other two sons. But I had come late into this family dynamic, and it was obvious Kayan's mother had a huge hold on him. So, we walked and walked.

"We're going to my sister's house," Kayan announced, then turned back and yelled something in Persian at a dark shadow following us.

"Kayan, who is it?"

"My mother."

The whole thing was eerie, but what I recognized was that my husband was taking a stand against someone who had a terrible control over him.

We arrived at a door, and Kayan banged on it with his fist. In the distance, I could see the dark shadow of Kayan's mother, her black chador fluttering in the breeze.

The door opened and inside was Kayan's brother-in-law and oldest sister, Fariba, whom I had only met briefly when I first arrived. I stood there quietly while Kayan explained our presence. I didn't like having others making decisions for me, and now it seemed like that was all I could do. Fariba and her husband parted, making way for us to pass between them and enter the house.

Inside the dark home were signs that the end of the day had passed long ago: folded laundry on a chair, washed dishes on a counter, toys and remnants of child's play.

Fariba led us down a hallway to a bedroom. Kayan and Fariba spoke in a hushed tone while Fariba shook her two daughters out of a deep slumber and guided their sleep-drenched bodies out of the room. We could hear Kayan's mother outside the door, crying and whining to whomever would listen.

Fariba made us a bed on the floor. It was still warm from where the little ones had slept. Kayan was fuming as we lay down on the bed. We didn't sleep; we just lay there curled up against one another, not saying a word. Sleep never came. My head was swirling with confusing thoughts, reliving the scene of Kayan tearing apart his family's home and the gun lying on the table next to him. And if that wasn't enough to think about, here we were lying in a child's bed with Kayan's mother outside our door. No, there were no words.

In the morning, the light shone through the window. I could hear movement throughout the house. There was a tap at the door. It was Fariba pleading for us to join her in the kitchen. The rest of the family had gone. We had missed the awkwardness of explaining our presence to anyone who wanted details. I was sure the stage had been set for what was to come next. I kept looking to see if Kayan's mother was lurking behind something, ready to reattach to her son at any given moment.

Two cups of tea and an arrangement of Persian sweets were waiting for us on the table. I felt like it was a setup. Tempting us with treats. I didn't want to touch anything; I didn't want to cross over into what was potential enemy territory. Sharing a child's bed on the floor was one thing, but nourishment meant something much too familiar.

Kayan must have had the same feeling. He just sat there listening to his sister tearfully pleading with him, tears falling at all the right moments. Interesting how much you can understand even if it's in another language. I knew Kayan's sister wanted all this to go away. She desperately wanted to heal the relationship between Kayan and their mother.

I waited for Kayan's reaction. He slipped his hand into mine like all the other times, and I heard his words in anger back to Fariba. They were strong and powerful. We stood up in protest. I watched their response to each other to see if we were leaving as friends or enemies. We marched to the front door and stepped outside to a new day. Kayan's sister looked at me with an annoyed expression. I can't say it didn't hurt a bit even if it was hard for me to grasp the meaning of her look. I would soon have to adjust to my new role in the family dynamics as Kayan's evil wife. Now everyone hated me, except the only one who mattered—Kayan. They needed a scapegoat; who better than the American wife?

Kayan and I walked, knowing we had to return to his home. We avoided the feeling of defeat by talking about our plans for the future. First, we would see if we could get a visa for Kayan to leave. When he had tried to leave before, so many people were fleeing the country they closed the borders, and he was trapped. We understood if we couldn't get a visa for him, we would have to illegally cross the border into Turkey. Once we had our papers, we would be able to enter the United States. It was risky. Very, very risky.

XVIII

ISFAHAN

That day we entered Kayan's home with a new mission. His mother stayed away from us and Kayan went off to work as if nothing had changed. At night we ate in our room, sharing plans about how we would leave, until one evening when Ahmed burst into our room panicked and out of breath. Tala was right behind him.

"Kayan, they are coming for Lara!" Tala blurted out while Ahmed yelled at Kayan in Persian.

It turned out not all the neighbors were supportive of having an American living amongst them, and rumors were spreading about what should be done with the American.

The idea Kayan had that I would be safe in Iran as his wife had turned out to be an impossibility. Iran wasn't the same home he had known. Two wars and new Islamic leadership had changed everything. There was no safe place for an American in Iran—not even for the wife of one of their own.

I'd never seen Ahmed so animated; his usual cool attitude was nonexistent in his conversation with Kayan.

My mind flew in all directions. One of the directions, strangely enough, was to get Kayan's gun to protect myself. How quickly I had gone from fear of guns to, "I'm going to need more than just one!"

Tala held on to my hand tightly. I had become her beloved sister-in-law, whom she was determined to keep. She was a child living in chaos, and I wished I could take her away from it all.

I tugged on Kayan's arm. "Kayan, we need to get out of here!"

I started throwing my belongings into my suitcase, Tala helping me. Kayan pulled that familiar green duffle bag out from under the table and started filling it with his clothes. He handed me his passport and a stack of official-looking papers.

"You hang on to these and hide the passport. Hide yours too!"

Kayan's mother was waiting at the bottom of the stairs. She grabbed hold of Kayan, trying to not let him pass. A rage like I had never seen poured out of him, and he yanked himself from his mother's grip. She threw her body in front of the gates. Ahmed stepped in and pulled his mother away, cursing at her. We dragged whatever we had and ourselves out into the night. Ahmed and Tala ran to catch up to us, protectively following for a while before Kayan insisted they go back.

"No, Kayan, take me too!" Tala cried out.

Ahmed argued with Kayan for a while. He was losing a third brother.

I comforted Tala. "Tala, it's not safe. Please go home."

Tala pulled on my arm. "I don't want anyone to hurt you. I love you, Lara!" She flung herself into my arms, crying. I wiped the tears from her cheeks. Amidst all the rushing she had managed to grab her chador. She held it out for me to take.

I looked at Kayan. He said nothing. I took the mass of black yardage and allowed Tala to drape it over my head and face.

"Look down." Tala directed me to look at the ground so no one would see the color of my eyes.

I kissed her on the forehead and hugged Ahmed. Ahmed stiffened, still not comfortable with open affection.

"Go!" Kayan pointed for them to leave.

They stood in the darkness, watching us walk away. I tried not to look back, afraid it would be an invitation for them to join us. We walked what seemed to be miles. I figured out much of the walking was Kayan's way of deciding our next move.

"We'll go to my sister Maryam's home in Isfahan. I wanted to take you there anyway. It's a small town. My brother-in-law is in the army and they live on the base where we'll be safe."

"Kay, do you really think a military base is the place to go?" I didn't like questioning his judgment, but I felt like I was being handed to the wolves.

"My brother-in-law is very highly regarded; it will be okay."

I dropped my bag and broke down crying. "I want to go home!"

My whole body shook as I stood in a dark alley with the realization that people wanted to hurt me. Not for anything I had done, but for who I was and what I represented. I had no way to change any of that, nor did I want to, and yet here I was hiding under a veil.

Kayan held me in his warm arms, and as insane as my world had become, the bad faded as he held me.

I sniffled and wiped the tears away. For the moment I was done. I didn't know or understand any of what was going on around me. There was nothing in my past that had prepared me for the events that were happening. Quite the contrary; everything I had experienced up until now had been idyllic. I had a near-perfect childhood, a loving family, and a government that made me feel safe. But I was getting all too good at flipping into survival mode and pushing all outside conditions out of my mind.

I could choose another day to reminisce, but right now I just wanted to stay alive.

Kayan had me wait in the doorway of a closed shop while he tried to get a taxi, which wasn't easy. There was very little nightlife to keep them in business, and hanging out on a corner waiting for one wasn't wise.

A taxi pulled up next to Kayan. It was already filled with two other passengers; it was not uncommon for taxis to pick up as many passengers as possible, especially with gas rationing.

Kayan opened the back door where two men were seated.

When the driver saw me, he did a double take. At least with the chador I got a double take. The driver began arguing with Kayan, making it clear he didn't want me in his cab. Kayan ignored the driver's request and waved me over, pushing me into the back seat with the other passengers. They quickly jumped out and moved to the front, making room for us. I slumped down next to Kayan.

Exasperated, the driver took off, quickly racing up and down the narrow alleys.

The other passengers started a conversation with Kayan. The driver banged his finger on a handmade sign taped to the dashboard of his car. Everyone went silent.

Kayan explained, "The sign says no politics spoken in the taxi. Everyone is always complaining, and he doesn't want to hear it all day."

The driver nodded, looking at me in the rearview mirror, and smiled. *Not a bad guy*, I thought, even though he'd been throwing me out of his taxi minutes before.

Kayan looked at me. "We can take a bus to Isfahan. They don't stop running until 8:00. We should make it."

The only words I heard were, "We should make it."

Suddenly, the driver yanked the cab to the side of the road, throwing us up against one another. Everyone started yelling in Persian and panic filled the cab. Bright lights shined through the windshield. As the lights got closer, we could see mobs of people carrying torches and moving towards us. Kayan ordered everyone to lock their doors.

The driver desperately tried to turn the cab around, which trapped it between other cars.

"Kayan!" I screamed.

Kayan pulled my head down towards him, covering me with the chador. "Stay down until they pass!"

My heart pounded inside my chest. I could see the demonstrators angrily walking around the car, hitting and rocking the cab. The door handles angrily jiggled from side to side. Hands slapped up against the windows. There was loud, angry chanting, and they used fire from torches to see the taxi's interior. I almost thought they would feel the adrenaline pumping inside the cab or see the fear on our faces. But miraculously, the demonstrators missed seeing me inside.

The irony was that they were demonstrating for peace. They carried banners and had fake blood splattered on their white t-shirts. Their faces were twisted in anger over having lost whatever freedoms they once had before the new regime. I understood it all. If it had been me, I'd be right there demonstrating with them. But this was not my war or my country, so instead, I hid in the back seat of the taxi, praying that I would not be seen by these peace marchers—praying that our next step, whatever that would be, would free us from the frightening life-and-death nightmare we had found ourselves in.

To our surprise, the driver turned out to be our ally and was quite an experienced driver. At some point, he had had enough and veered the car onto the sidewalk. I could see marchers trying to escape the taxi. It was funny how in an instant we had gone from victims to being the threat. I liked our new role much better. We weaved in and out of the demonstrators and found ourselves on the dark streets of Tehran.

It was eerily quiet; there were no lights because of the mandatory blackout, and most of the city's citizens had long before locked themselves in their homes. The inside of the cab was silent now. The experience with the demonstrators had left everyone numb with fear.

Kayan kept looking nervously at his watch. He called something out to the driver, who responded by driving faster. Fortunately, there were no other cars to slow us down. The driver was enjoying his new challenge. However, the other passengers were frozen in their seats. It was not the ride home they were expecting. Like a stuntman in action, the driver flew onto the sidewalk and delivered us to a bus parked on the street with its engine running.

We jumped out of the taxi and ran to the bus. I looked back to see the driver giving us a thumbs up. Universal language.

Kayan banged on the door of the bus. The driver looked at me and, without even a double take, started to pull away.

In a very brave or foolish move, Kayan ran in front of the bus and held his arms out. The annoyed bus driver reluctantly stopped and opened the bus door. Kayan mumbled something that I'm sure was not nice to the driver as we moved towards the back of the bus. Thankfully, the bus was empty—no glares from other passengers to avoid.

As the night went on, others did board, so I hunkered down, pulling the chador around me for cover, hoping no one would notice me. Kayan was braver and shared a conversation or two with other passengers. I wished I had the same freedom. I watched and listened, getting pieces of the stories they shared. Most of them were political while some were about the war. I knew Kayan had a few of those himself.

We rode all night, sleeping wrapped up in one another. I didn't want daylight to come. Hiding was much easier in darkness. With the arrival of a new day, life got serious—sometimes very serious. I discovered adrenaline pumping through my body had become a plus. There was less thinking and more movement towards a solution. Even if it was wrong or short-lived, it was movement towards a goal.

I wrestled with thoughts that did make their way through. How long could Kayan keep trying to protect me? The outside world was not going away. The day would come when he wouldn't be there, and then what? What a terrible burden he had in protecting me. The worst part of all was that there was nothing I could do to change it. I watched Kayan sleep instead, remembering all those months I had longed to wake up next to him. Cramped up against the window of the bus, he looked peaceful. His eyes began to focus as I stroked his arm, a smile appearing on his face before sleep overtook him again.

The bus pulled to a stop. Kayan opened his eyes, looked around, and stretched like a bear being awoken from a winter's hibernation.

"This is it, Isfahan!" Kayan said, pointing out the window. "That's the Great Mosque of Isfahan I wanted you to see. The military base is very close by."

Outside the window there were tall trees and a large lawn surrounding the mosque. Everything was green, no gray soot anywhere. Kayan pulled me out of my seat, laughing at my awkward attempt to wrap the chador around me. I learned there were rules to the process of wearing a chador. In order to hide myself, I would need to learn to do it perfectly. In the meantime, I wore a disheveled look, one side rising higher than the other and only a small square of fabric left to cover my face. I could hear Tala's words: "Look down." Yet another challenge—learning to navigate from here to there without looking where I was going. Kayan's gentle lead helped. Once again, I had to give up control.

Exiting the bus, I pulled him in the direction of the lawn rather than the paved pathways. "This feels so good, Kayan."

"I knew you'd like it here. Maybe we could live in Isfahan!" Kayan said, excited by the promise of something positive.

We slowly walked to the front of the beautiful mosque. We walked slowly because there really was something special about this place, and it wasn't just the green lawn. At the moment it transcended all thought; it was peace. A huge, blue, mosaic-tiled dome sat on top of one of the buildings. Underneath were tiled arches, walkways, and rooms all laden with small tiles creating pictures and colorful designs. There was scaffolding, and workers were busy expanding on what was already there. The artwork and detail was stunning.

Kayan took on the role of my tour guide. "They've been working on the mosque for over 1,000 years. It's always under construction, always growing."

"Kind of like people," I added.

Kayan looked at me and smiled. "I guess so."

For a moment or two we felt normal in this mosque built in the 11th, century in a town called Isfahan. Then there was a sudden crash that caused me to jump. Without a thought, I immediately hid myself by looking down at the ground. A worker scurried down the scaffolding to retrieve a hand tool that he had dropped. Kayan gave me a reassuring smile, and I gave him one back.

Amidst the tourists and workers were people kneeling and praying. Some laid out small rugs to kneel on and reached up to the heavens, with beads in their hands.

"The tasbih," I whispered to Kayan, which made him smile again. Like open arms, the mosque welcomed us to its calming center. Maybe it was the 1,000 years' worth of prayers it held. I squeezed Kayan's hand, and for the next few moments we joined the many who had stood where we were and quietly prayed, adding two more prayers to the mosque. On our way out, we again crossed the lawn. I walked over and touched the trunk of a big olive tree, knowing it had stories to tell me.

Kayan leaned into my ear. "We should go. The military base is about a mile from here."

I looked at Kayan sadly, not wanting to give up the moment, not knowing when I would feel that peace again. Normally he would have thrown me over his shoulder, or I would have jumped on his back, calling out, "Faster!" But it seemed I had already adapted to some of the new mores. I'm not sure if it was the culture or the fear of retribution for stepping out of line. The changes didn't go unnoticed for either of us.

We slowly crossed the lawn, my head down, while Kayan signaled for a taxi. Though it would have been an easy walk, neither of us felt safe having me walking on the streets. Our taxi joined the long line of other cars and trucks waiting to enter the base.

There was an irony in our entering a military base to find refuge. By now I had learned not everyone in a uniform was my friend. As we pulled up, soldiers immediately flanked the car on all sides. One barked orders at the driver, never taking his gaze off of me. The chador hid nothing from him. Kayan handed the driver our passports and nervously explained our purpose of being there. The guard abruptly turned and entered his armored shack.

Here I am, I thought, *again waiting to pass someone's approval.* It seemed like that was all I'd done since I entered the Middle East. Everything about me needed approval, and any kind of approval was given reluctantly. If it wasn't my passport or paperwork, it was my belongings or me. Mostly it was me. How was I going to be perceived by these soldiers at the gate whose sole purpose was to keep their military base safe?

We watched the guard through the glass window of the shack. He was animated at first, nervously flipping our passports in his hand. In frustration, he picked up a phone. Obviously, he needed support.

The phone was a big, black, chunky one and reminded me of the one in the phone booth Superman used before facing some major catastrophe. Were we this man's catastrophe? In my head, I saw us being cross-examined by brutal military under hot, bright lights, with maybe an electrical device to shock us if they didn't like our answers. Maybe we would make a run for it and get shot in the back for being spies!

To our surprise, the soldier returned and handed Kayan our passports and a map showing us where to go with a big X covering a building. Although we breathed a sigh of relief, there was a part of me thinking they had made a mistake. Did they not see that I was an American? Surely something was wrong. I was used to being far more important than being handed a map with an X on it. Why, I'd singlehandedly unnerved a five-star general, for God's sake! I'd sent armed bandits back to the hills from which they came and evaded hundreds at a packed bazaar! These people had no idea what they were dealing with.

Kayan shook the map in my face, bringing me back to the present moment. "I think we're lost," he said.

The base was huge and went on farther than we could see. Large steel fencing surrounded everything with razor sharp wiring at the top. There would be no escaping from here.

Kayan explained the tall buildings were apartments housing the soldiers who lived and worked on the base. He was familiar with the base because he had visited his sister when he first came back to Iran.

"Everything is beige," I said.

The base was in the barren desert and everything was desert beige.

"They don't want to stand out and become the enemy's target," Kayan said, covering my hand with his.

This was yet another reality check as to where I was and the realities of the world around me; it was quite different than the beauty and peace of the mosque only blocks away. Everywhere we looked, military soldiers were headed to their destinations. Their beige army fatigues blended with the desert background as well. Their movements were stiff and deliberate, but most didn't carry the usual weapons I was used to seeing. I guess they were already protected by just being there.

Kayan looked at Isfahan as a potential home for us. It was much smaller, with little to no chaos like that of Tehran. Along the way, we'd discussed a plan to first stay with his sister and her family before finding jobs and our own home. It all sounded good, but I wasn't sure I was willing to bite into that apple. Too much had preceded this moment. My former naïve self had been awakened, and I didn't know if I could forget all that had happened. Escaping Tehran the night before still played out in my thoughts.

My current plan was to simply stay alive. *Wow, how crazy is that?*

A couple loops around the base and, with the help of Kayan's past recollection, we arrived in front of a tall, beige cinderblock apartment building. We got out of the cab and stood looking up with our suitcases in hand.

"You'll like my sister Maryam. She's older, but we were always close."

Kayan grabbed both our suitcases and started climbing the outside cement stairs. I followed behind, carrying the smaller bags.

"What floor does she live on?" I asked, praying it was the first.

"She's on the 15th."

"Can't we take the elevator?" I asked.

Kayan laughed. "If there was one. I was afraid to tell you, but there is no elevator and technically, it's 30 flights of stairs. I counted last time. I can always come back down and pick up the bags."

"You know, Kayan, you have a lot of 'I was afraid to tell yous.' Is there anything else I should know?"

"That I love you so much, and we are going to have a wonderful life together, I promise."

He gave me that boyish smile, the one where both his dimples raised a bit. That was the smile he gave when he was desperate to get his way, and the smile that always worked!

By the time we reached his sister's door, we both were huffing and puffing. Kayan knocked and two little boys opened the door. They looked at him and then at me and ran off screaming for their mother. His sister rushed to the door with warm, high-energy greetings, which seemed to melt away when she greeted me.

"Lara, this is my sister Maryam, and these two are Jahan and Mansour. You are their aunt."

I just let that lay there.

The apartment was furnished in French Provincial. The couch and matching chairs were covered in dark green velvet, and toys were scattered throughout, adding just a touch of chaos. Kayan wrestled with the little ones. I could tell they were very happy to see their uncle. But towards me, they had a healthy stay-away-she-is-different reaction. They had most likely never seen someone who was not like them and dealt with it by pretending I was not in the room. I didn't take offense.

Maryam offered all the niceties—tea, food, and candies on small pink flowered plates. I reminded myself that she'd had no idea we were coming and of how gracious she was for being surprised by two guests. I slipped off my chador before we all sat at the table and sipped our tea. Maryam tried to communicate with me through Kayan. It was an empty conversation, and then we found out why. Our showing up had not surprised her at all. They had a phone, and Kayan's mother had gone to a neighbor's house to call and fill her in on what had taken place at home. We had walked into an ambush! Like a loyal daughter, Maryam had immediately taken the side of her mother.

Even with the language barrier, I understood what was going on between Kayan and his sister. They had heated words. Kayan stood his ground, and whenever Maryam looked in my direction, she immediately looked away as if to say, "You mean nothing to me"—which was true. Kayan and I had been living our lives on our own for over five years, and in all those years, never had it occurred to us that we needed to ask anyone other than ourselves permission to live our lives the way we wanted.

For the time being, Kayan and his sister tabled their argument. Maryam showed us to a bedroom with bedrolls already laid out for us. Of course they were. Just like in Kayan's home, on top of a dresser sat the two pictures of Ali and Sergis with a small candle burning next to them. Maryam walked over and blew out the candle. I could feel the tension between us. I began to feel like the other woman in a threesome.

Kayan showed me to the bathroom, and there it was sitting against one wall: a gleaming white porcelain toilet. I smiled at Kayan.

He laughed. "You're so easy to please."

On another wall was a showerhead and faucet. The entire bathroom from one side to the other had white tiles and morphed into a shower with a drain in the middle of the floor.

Kayan slowly started to remove my clothes. I pulled away.

"Scram! There are two children on the other side of that door!"

"I locked the door," he said confidently.

I laughed and pointed for him to leave. He lowered his head like a sad child. "We are never having children!" Kayan said in an authoritative voice and left the room.

Later that evening, Maryam's husband, Valentin, came home. He was dressed in military fatigues. His presence set the room on fire. Right in front of our eyes, Maryam became the dutiful wife, taking her husband's lunchbox and coat. She was no longer playing the role of the strong woman telling her younger brother what to do. I liked this new Maryam better than the last one. The kids flew around the room, each trying to get their father's attention, which they did. He spun them around, encouraging them to compete with one another. Another interesting dynamic.

Kayan introduced me to Valentin. He kindly held out his hand to shake mine, welcoming me to his home. It felt sincere. I actually felt welcomed.

We had a nice dinner. I could tell Maryam had gone out of her way to make it nice, and it was. After dinner, the men sat on the couch and talked while Maryam and I cleaned up the kitchen.

Maryam didn't try to connect with me, and although I would have loved a confidant, I knew immediately she would not be the one. She had drawn the line in the sand before we got there and, in my naïveté, I hadn't even recognized there was a war. I'm sure if I had understood the language, I would have known to come armed.

Over the next few days, we hid out at Kayan's sister's home. Kayan insisted we were just visiting, but we both knew the truth. The good part was we were able to be with one another. We'd missed each other so much. But it didn't take long to come to the reality that this could not go on forever. There was no life outside the apartment, and although it was obvious Maryam loved her brother, it was equally as obvious that she did not like me.

One afternoon I asked Kayan to go for a walk. He hesitated, and I knew why. He didn't want to look at the reality. The current pretending was keeping us safe and, more importantly, together. But he agreed, and we bravely walked down the 30 flights of stairs. I had poorly wrapped myself in the chador and had to be careful not to trip over the dragging garment. With each step I reminded myself I'd be climbing up that same step to get back into the apartment—the dilemma—but it was worth it. There was fresh air, something we had not had since we arrived.

Outside, we were surrounded by row after row of tall apartment buildings and cement sidewalks that ran everywhere but led nowhere. Maybe they were waiting for the future to be built. In the meantime, Kayan and I found taking a walk a challenge. Sometimes the path led us with the promise of something great at the end, and then nothing. We laughed, comparing it to our current situation.

We immediately made it a game, competing to see which one of us could choose the longest path. We looked like five-year-olds on a playground, laughing and pushing each other off the sidewalk. I rarely won at these games but enjoyed every second.

In the distance, we could see soldiers carrying on with their duties. We kept our conversation just a little over a whisper so as not to attract attention. Realizing there was nowhere for us to go, we circled back in front of the apartment building, trying to look casual. We didn't. I looked at Kayan in the saddest way. I loved him like no other person in my life. It wasn't simply that we completed each other; it was more like that feeling you get when you are down to the last piece of a puzzle and it fits. We just fit. One of the great things about us was we didn't always need words. We knew what the other thought and felt. Right now, it was fear and a lot of confusion.

"Let's go home, Lara."

I spun around, looking at Kayan, making sure the words had really come from him.

"Are you sure, Kayan? What about...?"

"What about what? My world will not let us be together. We tried; we have no other choice."

"And your mother? What about her?" I asked.

"She has my brother and sisters. She'll be fine."

I loved hearing his words. Each one gave me a beautiful sense of well-being, a beam of light in what had been so much darkness. The plan was we would return to Tehran and see if we could get the proper paperwork for Kayan to leave the country. My American passport should be enough for me. We were prepared to find another way if our plan didn't work.

XIX

LAND MINES

The next morning, we said our goodbyes to our hosts. Although no words were said about it, our plan was not a secret—and sure enough, when we returned to Kayan's home, his mother was waiting with a mix of tears and anger. I tried so hard not to judge this woman, reminding myself that she had lost two sons. But the one thing I could not tolerate was unkindness, and she was incredibly unkind to her son.

It would take a lifetime to undo the words she had thrust upon him. I wondered if she was always that unkind or if it was the result of the hurt and pain she was living with. Either way, I avoided her. Tala and Ahmed were happy to see us back and welcomed us as if we had gone on vacation and not run away to save my life.

Kayan directed everyone to tell all the neighbors that I had gone back to the United States. He ran across a neighbor on the street who told him he was so sorry things did not work out for us. Kayan nodded and went on his way, pleased with his accomplishment.

After work, Kayan hurried off to a variety of government offices to see what he could do to leave the country. He was bounced from one office to another, all with the same outcome. There were no visas being issued at that time. He returned worn out both physically and emotionally.

The United States had closed its doors after the hostage situation. Anyone coming from Iran would most likely not be let in, and there still wasn't an American Embassy in Iran to help. Kayan was an Iranian citizen with an Iranian passport. Being married to an American qualified him for citizenship in the United States, but changing his citizenship had never been a thought until now.

He slapped a handful of papers in his hands authoritatively. "That's it. The decision on how we leave has been made for us. We'll have to illegally cross the Turkish border."

I looked at Kayan, waiting for him to fill in all my racing questions. Just like always, without my even asking, he addressed each one. The answers weren't satisfying—frightening, really. I had now been to Turkey and

I had been to Iran. Choosing one over the other was a hard choice; neither was a good one for me. Once we crossed the Turkish border, my passport would get me home. With Kayan's Iranian passport and our marriage certificate, Kayan should be able to get home as well. At least that was the plan. It was all we had. We also acknowledged that it may take us a few days while we waited in Turkey for the government to figure out what to do with us. Fortunately, they had an American Embassy.

Ideally, we would pay someone in Iran to drive us to the Turkish border. From there we'd have to physically hike across.

"None of those fancy shoes, Lara. It's rough terrain. Make sure you wear something you can hike and climb in."

Those words swirled in my head. Hike and climb while sneaking into a foreign country...

"I have to say goodbye to my family, Lara. I can't disappear without saying goodbye."

I nodded, leery but understanding.

That night, for the first time since we'd left the house, we all sat down to eat together. We sat there like nothing had ever happened. The holes on the wall were a reminder of something different. To say I was anxious was an understatement. Every time Kayan spoke in Persian, I wondered if that was it. Was he telling his family goodbye?

And just about the time I relaxed, forgetting the job at hand, Kayan's mother let out a shriek and a booming, "Na!", which I knew meant no. She stood up, pacing the floor, looking at Kayan and waving her arms as if she had gone mad. Kayan spoke softly to her, trying to calm her down, but this was her golden moment and she wasn't about to give it up.

I reached for Kayan's arm instinctively, trying to be supportive and needing something to hold on to. I wasn't used to this kind of explosiveness, and I didn't know where this woman would take things. After all, she had already blamed her son for the death of his brother. What terribly cruel thing could she do or say next?

Kayan's mother began to fall apart in front of us. She cried and held her hands over her heart, then raised them as if pleading to God. Kayan started to cry, but not the kind of crying one does when they're sad. It was more like a deep grieving. His mother had gotten what she had worked so hard for. All the anger that Kayan and his mother had felt before had stepped aside. What remained was two people in raw pain. Everyone else in the room was silently watching as things evolved. Kayan turned to me, trying to hold back the tears.

"My mother says she will die if I leave, and it will be my fault."

Kayan's mother paced, holding her hands to her chest and repeating the word "Allah" over and over. In that moment, I didn't know what happened, but I understood why Kayan had tried to tear down the walls of his family home. I felt his head fall on my shoulder and his tears soak through my shirt. At some point, we stood up and retreated to our room like we were 16 again. Most of that night was a huge, gigantic blur. Kayan was a mess.

All I knew to do was love him. So, I held him through the night, and in the morning, we stayed in our bed on the floor and let all the feelings out. It was obvious to both of us that Kayan could not walk out carrying the burden his mother had laid on him.

Did I think it was right or correct? No. I felt he was choosing his mother over us, over me, over our marriage. I felt hurt, anger, disbelief, and so many other dramatic and painful things. But after being in Iran and living amongst this family, I also had an understanding of something I would not have normally understood.

An understanding that meant I was going home alone.

Kayan held on to me like a treasured keepsake. As unbelievably painful as this moment was, we both knew this was what our future was going to be. There was little understanding, and all the analyzing was not going to change the fact that Kayan was unable to live with the guilt of something happening to his mother because of him.

Our dream of living in Iran was an impossibility. As much as I loved Kayan, I was not going to give up my life to ease his guilt or make his mother happy.

Lots of pieces started falling into place. If I were to be honest with myself, I would have to admit that the hold Kayan's mother and family had over him had always been present; I just never knew or experienced it from 8,000 miles away. I was grateful for the distance that all those years had given us and the loving innocence and life we'd safely shared. It was truly the greatest gift of all. Did this change who Kayan was or my love for him? That was impossible.

I was numb with feelings, and my primary goal now was to get home safely. Any healing I had to do would have to happen there.

The next day, Kayan and I struggled with our feelings and the logistics of my leaving. The only flight out of Iran that week would be the following day. We would have to get a ticket at the airport because of the short notice. My visa had not expired, so we were good on that end.

"You could stay longer. No one knows you're here, Lara." Kayan didn't hear or understand what he had just said.

"I can't stay hidden in your home for the rest of my life, Kayan. Besides, what if someone does find out and decides to make a political statement by harming me? Can you protect me from what's out there?"

Kayan lowered his head, acknowledging what he was asking of me. For the first time, he also acknowledged that he could not keep me safe. As long as I lived in Iran, I would never be safe.

When I was a child, I read and loved the book *The Diary of Anne Frank*. It was the story of a young Jewish girl and her family who were hidden from the Germans in a neighbor's house during the war. Anne had created an entire world in the attic where they hid, and her only crime was being Jewish. I did have a choice. I could live my life with Kayan locked up and hidden in this house, praying that no one would find out I was there, or I could live a full life back home without Kayan, the man I loved with every ounce of my being. I knew Kayan would have liked me to be happy locked away in this house, relying on him to share the outside everyday world, to be his Anne Frank kept in this room waiting for him to come home, but he also knew I deserved to live a full life, filled with all the good the world had to give. He loved me selfishly on the outside, but unselfishly on the inside.

Knowing our reality and accepting it was a challenge for both of us. Just the thought of not having Kayan in my life was devastating. So, I kept my mind on the task of leaving Iran.

That night we stayed alone in our room; every minute was precious. I'm not going to lie and pretend I didn't have any resentment towards Kayan—beginning with the question of why he couldn't stand up to his mother, walk out the door with me, and wish her well. I had a long list of resentments. I resented Kayan's brothers for having been the catalyst for everything that was happening. I resented them for dying and all the pain they had caused. I resented the country for all the hate it spewed. I resented the judgment people cast on me, not through knowing me, but to use me as a scapegoat for everything bad that had ever happened to them. Mostly, I resented life not turning out the way I had wanted it to.

Kayan walked up behind me, moving my hair to one side of my neck and kissing it ever so gently. Would this be the last time he would kiss me that way?

"I love you so much, Lara. What will I do without you in my life?"

He picked me up, spinning me around. I loved it. I always thought I was too heavy to be picked up, but Kayan did it effortlessly. Tears dropped down my cheeks and onto his. We made love that night. It was different, not at all like the fun we used to have sharing each other's bodies. It was a mixture of *I don't want the intimacy* and *I want to love you one last time*, which was unimaginable. We fell asleep entangled in one another, Kayan's strong, muscular legs wrapped around me, pulling me into him and holding me tightly.

I woke up to the sound of Kayan lightly snoring in my ear. I never understood why people hated their partner's snoring. I loved the reminder I was not alone.

We both woke up knowing everything we did was for the last time. While Kayan went out to get us something to eat, I packed up all my belongings, some of which had become part of the room, like a small table I used to lay out my makeup and hair items. I had stopped wearing makeup after I arrived in the Middle

East. The incident at the bazaar had taught me quickly not to stand out. There were stories that after the regime change, women were assaulted for wearing makeup. One story conveyed that men would cut a woman's lips with a razor blade for wearing lipstick. It was apparent that the religious fanatics had given themselves the power to decide how others were to live their lives, especially women. Unfortunately, those fanatics were encouraged by the new regime.

Tala liked to come to our room and play with the makeup and hair items on the table. As if she was playing dress-up, she would ask me to teach her how to use the different tubes and bottles. We enjoyed being girls together. I was by far not the only victim of this religious government, and I always made sure Tala took off every trace of makeup before she left the room. It was our little secret.

Looking at the makeshift table now, there was a part of me that wanted to leave the items for Tala, but the fear of anyone finding out and hurting her made me throw it all in my bag. I made sure to gather every little item in the room that was mine, as if I'd never been there. That's how I wanted to leave it.

Tala and Ahmed greeted Kayan and I at the bottom of the stairs. Tala was already crying, and surprisingly, Ahmed was not doing a very good job at trying to hold it together either. During our hugs and kisses, I could see Kayan's mother peering out from the downstairs bedroom. She was getting what she wanted. Kayan was staying her dutiful son and I was leaving. I will never understand the evil that possessed her—notwithstanding that she had lost two sons.

Kayan had to pry Tala off of me. I kissed her and a reluctant Ahmed on top of their heads. I always felt a kiss on the head was like an angel leaving a protective mark. With that, we left for the airport.

One last time, I draped the chador around myself, looked down at the ground, and walked through the teal gates. The taxi drive to the airport was quiet as Kayan and I sat in the back seat of the cab. We both sat still, occasionally sniffling and dabbing tears from the corners of our eyes. More than once I caught the driver looking at us in the rearview mirror. I started to feel angry. I wanted to yell, "Stop looking at me," but I didn't. How could I unleash all of this on some poor driver trying to make a living? Kayan and I had said all the words we had the night before; I had no more "I love yous" left. I wanted this ride to be over—until I looked at Kayan. Then, I never wanted it to end. As we drove through Tehran this time, Kayan was not the tour guide explaining the history of all the buildings, talking about how he mourned the ones no longer standing and remembering what they had meant to him. This ride was quiet and somber.

"I already miss you," he said in a slow, painful, barely audible whisper.

I squeezed his hand. I felt no excitement about going home. I loved my home and more than ever the privilege of living in my country, but going home meant I was saying goodbye to Kayan, for which I had no words. My mind felt like a rock tumbler, thoughts and emotions rolling about and bumping into one another, unable to escape the process of the tumbler itself.

The taxi pulled up to the front of the airport. There was a mad hustle of hundreds of people moving about. It was obvious they were on a mission, and I knew not to get in their way. Some were carrying what seemed to be every item they owned. Although they had the normal suitcases and bags, they also had boxes of household treasures like paintings in gold frames, statues obviously of value, and carpets. Most were carrying Persian carpets rolled tightly and tied with straw twine.

Kayan explained that after the coup, people started fleeing from Iran. Anyone having any connection to the Shah could be imprisoned and tried as a traitor, an enemy of the people. Iran pulled no punches. People were publicly executed, beaten, and tortured in retaliation by Khomeini's new regime. Those who fled tried to carry everything they could that had any monetary value and would help them start a new life elsewhere. The Persian government deliberately closed its borders and was restrictive on what could be taken—only two Persian rugs and small amounts of jewelry, cash, etc. Like drug smugglers, people hid items of value, hoping they could sneak them out of the country.

Many had had their bank accounts frozen; this was the government's way of keeping the economy from being destroyed. Iran was being recreated by its new regime from the ground up.

"They're not leaving Iran, they're fleeing," Kayan said, pulling me to his side and away from the stampede.

So, I wasn't the only one fleeing Iran. Everyone had his or her own reasons for leaving the country. For some it was economic; others were afraid of being persecuted for having been a part of the previous government, and many, just like myself, were escaping the judgment and prejudice of the new regime. Chaos was the best word to describe the inside of the airport. Hundreds of people trying to leave the country on the only day of the week that Iran Air was allowed to fly one plane out. All other airlines had been banned from flying into or out of Iran.

Inside the airport, huge banners of Khomeini hung on every wall, reminding you who was in control. Kayan held my hand tightly as we moved through the crowd, his protective eyes never leaving me. I was bumped and pushed around, but this time it wasn't personal. It was necessary in this environment, a given. Most everyone was moving in one direction or another. We simply got swept up in the movement.

Kayan pulled me to his side. "We need to go through security first."

He said it as if I had never been through security before, and then I reminded myself he had missed that whole leg of my journey. I nodded, acknowledging what he had said as we joined a security checkpoint with women and children lined up on one side and men on the other. I saw Kayan give the women next to me a kind look and a few Persian words. They acknowledged me and smiled. Kayan kissed me on my head and whispered, "Love you. I'll be right over there." He scooted my suitcase next to me and pointed to a line of men waiting to go through their checkpoint. Before I could respond, I felt his hand slip away from mine. The women around me smiled kindly, letting me know I was with them.

The people who were most likely leaving their country forever fascinated me. Some were quietly doing whatever was asked of them. Others were weeping, their eyes watching loved ones walk away, not knowing if they'd ever see one another again.

But most seemed to be in survival mode, doing whatever they had to do to leave Iran. They were strong and in control, monitoring their children and their belongings as the lines slowly moved forward. You could tell these women were in a fight for their lives, with an unknown fate waiting for them in their new home.

I replayed the stories Kayan had told me about how the Shah gave his private secret service, SAVAK, the authority to do whatever they needed in the guise of protecting the country. That sometimes included dragging people out of their homes if someone heard or felt they were a threat. Some would never be heard from again; others were locked up and interrogated in torturous ways or held before judges in mock courts. The bottom line—there was no freedom or justice.

However, the new regime seemed no better. In many ways, it was much worse because everything they did was in the name of Allah and Mohammed, whom they believed to be the final prophet of God. Anything done in the name of Mohammed seemed to get a free pass in the new society. I wondered, *If Mohammed were here today, would he be supportive of the things being done in his name, like so many other atrocities done in the name of a religion?*

I knew I'd never know the answer to many of my questions, but I couldn't help but think about what all this was really about as I stood in line with hundreds of others, frightened over a religious right. Many said it was about oil; Iran had lots of it. Others called it a religious battle, a fight against the evils of modernization.

An argument going on in my line caught my attention. It was between airline security and a woman draped in an unusually large black chador, holding the hand of a small child. At one point in the midst of their argument, I watched as the child was actually lifted off the ground by his mother's flailing arms! The child cried and the mother shrieked and moaned, much like Kayan's mother had. The woman was moved out of the line and we all crept up a little faster.

When I entered the security checkpoint, two women in security outfits with hijabs tightly covering their heads approached me. Surprised to see I was an American, they stopped what they were doing. The women that Kayan had spoken to in line immediately stepped in, and whatever was said seemed to satisfy the security officers. I thanked them by nodding and pulled the chador tightly around my face, fooling no one.

My emotions were all over the place. One moment I felt the energy drain from my body and the deepest sadness sweep over me, knowing I was leaving Kayan. The next moment there was an almost business-like feeling stepping in to take care of the details of leaving Iran. It was an odd dance.

One of the female security officers took my suitcase and backpack. Opening them, she carefully lifted the clothing items with a wooden ruler, peering underneath and running her gloved hands around the lining, much like they did at the Turkish border. This time they were looking for jewelry or money being smuggled out of the country. If the items were valued over a certain dollar amount, people had a choice of leaving them behind or staying in the country with their belongings. Most got on the plane.

Stacked against one long wall were several mountains of valuables, now property of the Iranian government. The agent motioned me to follow her into a freestyle dressing room with a curtain over the front, and just like at the Turkish border, the woman had me hold out my arms while she patted me down. Having a stranger touching me had bothered me before—it was funny how quickly I adjusted. I had become a pro at being patted down. But it was definitely more of a challenge for them since I was wearing the chador. We stepped outside the dressing room, where the woman had me remove the boots I was wearing. They were tan, made of soft leather and lined with lamb's wool. I chose to wear them knowing they were the best for protection. I hadn't decided why my feet needed protecting, but they served me well crossing Turkey.

The woman ran her hands in and out of my boots; holding her hand in one of them, she looked up at me. "*Gam*," she shared, which I knew meant warm. This woman really liked my boots—a little too much. I held my hand out to take them. She didn't respond. Was she trying to force me to bribe her with my boots? What else had she taken from others trying to leave the country? We both stood there looking at one another, saying nothing.

A male security officer approached me holding out his hand. "Passport?"

The woman handed back my boots and quickly went back to the line. With my boots tucked under one arm, I grabbed my passport from my backpack and handed it to the officer. He looked it over scrupulously like everyone always had, then shook his head side to side in an annoyed fashion.

"I'm leaving the country!" I blurted out.

"Come!" The security officer motioned with his hand for me to follow him.

He walked quickly through the airport, taking me in a direction away from the planes. I looked longingly at the planes and then at this man who didn't know who he was dealing with! He was a little man, not because of his size, but because of who he was, obviously very insecure and in need of control.

I was emotionally drained in every sense of the word. I was losing my husband and the entire country hated me. I was tired of being examined, treated by everyone like I was a terrorist. I still didn't have a plane ticket and now I was barefooted! I was all those things but noticed I wasn't scared. After everything I had faced and endured, I was no longer frightened. I was pissed; I wanted out! This little man with his hand on his gun didn't scare me at all. He led me to a small glass enclosed office, sat behind the oldest, nastiest desk I had ever seen, and took a deep breath.

I remained by the door, ready to get on a plane.

He held up my passport. "No!"

"I am an American citizen and that is my passport!"

"No!" This man was shrinking right in front of me. I wasn't afraid.

I'd faced machine guns, rifles, handguns, and other weapons with no idea what they were, but at some point, they all aimed in my direction. Who did he think he was?

And then Kayan burst into the office, out of breath, speaking a mile a minute to the officer.

I was so angry I wanted to tell Kayan, "Don't worry, I got this." But he stepped in front of me, facing the little man. The two of them engaged in a discussion. I had no idea what was being said, but thought, *My husband will show him!* Within a minute or two Kayan turned and faced me without looking into my eyes. That was a first, not at all like him.

"Kayan, what is it?" I asked.

"He says the new Islamic law says if you are married to an Iranian citizen, you automatically become an Iranian citizen. Your American passport is no good in Iran and if you want to leave Iran, you need to get an Iranian passport."

All my thoughts seemed to freeze, but Kayan without mercy went on. "As an Iranian citizen you will have to apply for a visa to the United States. Unfortunately, as an Iranian citizen you may have the same problem I had—the United States not giving you a visa. He said it takes about five years to get a visa. I'm so sorry, Lara."

Kayan looked at the little man for confirmation of what he had just said. The little man nodded and held up his hand, showing five short stubby fingers. Kayan stepped in to grab me as my legs went limp and everything around me started to swirl, including that nasty desk. He led me to the chair sitting in front of the little security officer. When I'd entered the room, I had told myself I would not sit down. I was not going to be here long enough. Now I was folded up in the chair, unable to control my breath. While Kayan held me in the chair with one hand, I could hear him and the little man conversing. *Why isn't he yelling?* I thought. *Why isn't he taking this little man's office apart piece by piece?*

The little man stood up from behind his desk holding my passport in his hand. He stumbled to speak in English, looking only at Kayan and avoiding looking at my lifeless body across from him, even though the words were meant for me.

"I am supposed to take your passport. It's no good here." Kayan started to say something when the little man handed him my passport. "But I won't."

Kayan led me out of the office. I immediately broke down crying, pushing him away. I needed someone to blame for what was going on, and it might as well have been him!

The ride home was silent. Inside I was praying like crazy to any God to save me from having to return to that house and face Kayan's mother again. The last thing she would want was to see the person who had threatened to take her son away. I was sure she'd been jumping for joy after seeing Kayan take me to the airport.

XX

FIVE FINGERS

My prayers weren't answered that day. Maybe they were, but not in the way I wanted. Nothing had been the way either Kayan or I wanted since I'd arrived in the Middle East. I kept hearing those two words that had come from the little man: "Five years!"

That night I slept with my back to Kayan. It was the first time ever that I had turned away from him. It felt awful. I knew it wasn't right. I didn't understand why I was turning away from the one person I loved and who loved me. But my anger superseded logic. Throughout the night I felt Kayan touch me. Even with my anger, it felt good knowing he was beside me.

In the morning, Kayan prepared to set out with the intention of finding someone who could help get me out of the country.

"I want to go. It's me we're trying to save!" I raged.

Kayan pulled me into him. "I can't get anything done if I have to worry about your safety."

"I'll wear the biggest chador they make. No one will know!" I grabbed the chador off a chair and threw it over myself, covering my head. Kayan pulled me in front of the mirrored hutch. We both looked at my reflection. There was no hiding who I was. Even with my hair and face covered, my blue eyes seemed even bluer peering out from the small opening in the chador.

"I'll wear sunglasses and look at the ground." I was desperate and wanted Kayan's approval.

"It's too big of a risk, Lara. You could probably fool most, but what about that one? Remember, I told everyone in the neighborhood you had already gone back to the United States. For now, you're safe if you stay here. Don't leave the house!"

I watched him walk out of our room, noticing that the pictures of his brothers sitting on the table seemed to be looking at me.

"This is all your fault!" I screamed at the pictures, rolling up the chador in my hands and throwing it at them.

They both went flying in different directions. I paused, looking at the outcome of my anger. Hardly noteworthy. Placing blame only felt good for a moment. The truth was that when Kayan had asked me to come to Iran, neither of us had had any idea how people would react to me. We just wanted to continue sharing our lives together. The "where" seemed unimportant at the time; now it was everything. What could I have done differently? Listened to my family and not come to the Middle East? Turned around in Istanbul after learning there were no flights to Iran? But I didn't do any of those things. In fact, the turning back option had never occurred to me. The reality of the world we were in changed all that, not the love we had for each other. The cruel truth was our love wasn't going to change what people felt when they looked at me. For now, the only things that offered me safety were the walls of this house. The irony was that I was living with a woman who clearly hated me.

"Five years" kept replaying in my head. I felt angry, scared, defensive—all feelings that were new to me, and I wasn't wearing them well. I carefully picked up the pictures and used the fabric of the chador to wipe the accumulated dust from their frames before gingerly putting them back on the table.

I looked at the pictures of Kayan's brothers. "I'm sorry, none of this is your fault. I'm sorry I didn't get to meet you." I lit the candle under the pictures, hoping that would make up for my outburst.

I spent the rest of the day up on the roof, sitting in the sun and reading the one book I had brought, *Affirmations for Everyday Life*. This was hardly everyday life, and I have no idea why I had chosen to bring this particular book. I had seen it on my mother's bookshelf where she kept all her self-help guru stuff, and it was the perfect size to fit into my suitcase. I didn't know at the time how valuable the book would become. Affirmations were entirely new to me. The idea was to affirm what you wanted in life. It could be written down, spoken repeatedly, but most importantly, you had to think it and expect it to happen.

I picked up the book and decided I would do the only thing I had control over. I started writing down, "I will be able to safely leave Iran soon." I wanted to add "with Kayan," but he was making a different choice. I wrote the words over and over again, thinking if I kept writing them, somehow the powers that be would hear them and make it happen. Maybe Mohammed himself would take pity on me after seeing how cruelly I was being treated and right the wrong. It didn't matter. I now had something I could do.

I didn't share it with Kayan. Like Cyrus, he subscribed to the idea that if you can't see it, it's not real, and I needed a miracle that I couldn't see.

The rest of the day I worked at filling up the blank pages of my binder with my affirmation, praying in the warm sun on the roof and eating the pickled onions. At one point the young woman next door came out onto her roof to hang laundry. Seeing her before had excited me; now I hid behind the wall, afraid she'd turn me in as an American terrorist. I watched as she hung each item of clothing, trying to piece together who this woman was. I decided her husband was a laborer of some sort by the white t-shirts and khaki pants. It was obvious she was pregnant with their first child since there was no other children's clothing. She was also conservative, wearing below-the-knee dresses made of dark, heavy cloth—normal attire for many Persian women at that time. The garments had a way of flying in the littlest breeze, probably because there was so much extra fabric. They moved side to side as if embodied by a spirit of their own.

On the roof I also wrote letters home; it was hard pretending everything was great, not letting on that anything was wrong. I couldn't imagine keeping the secret for five years while I was trapped in this country. That news would especially be devastating to my mother, so I was extra careful choosing my words. She had a sixth sense about her, which had driven me crazy when I was young. She always knew when things weren't right and had a way of getting my secrets out of me. But this secret was one I would have to keep to myself, for her sake.

"Lara, are you up here?"

I quickly closed my notebook.

Kayan climbed up the stairs and stood over me. "What are you doing up here and why are you in the corner?"

"Shhh, we're not alone," I whispered. I pointed in the direction of the neighbor doing her laundry and pulled him down to join me in my corner.

"Hmmm, this is kind of exciting," Kayan said, kissing me.

I playfully pushed him away. "I've decided the neighbor is a Khomeini spy. I've been watching her all day."

"You're losing it, Lara."

"I'm a product of my environment," I snapped back.

Kayan looked at me, his eyes softening, then back at the neighbor now taking her laundry down. "What secrets does her laundry hold?" he quipped.

I missed this part of Kayan, his lightheartedness, the way he laughed at himself, the way we both laughed at ourselves. We thought we were hysterical. Even the difficult times could make us bust out laughing at the absurdity of a situation. Neither of us laughed much now.

In fact, the day I'd arrived and pried myself out of the taxi, Kayan had looked and, more importantly, felt different. He was pale and much thinner. He'd always had a strong body, but at that moment he looked as if he had been sick. I reminded myself of what he had just been through, not giving it much thought. After all, we were together now; everything was going to be okay. My eyes saw the Kayan I knew, the Kayan who was playful and fun, the Kayan I met on that beach years ago who had trouble standing on a surfboard and took advantage of innocent surfers in a game of soccer.

And now I understood why he'd felt different to me. He no longer lived in that world. This world was a hostile one that killed two of his brothers, that sent him to war and held him captive, emotionally and physically, a world that had no place for the person he was. There was no place for lightheartedness when the streets were lined with funerals and sirens warning of the threat of cities being bombed.

"Come here, my little spy." He pulled me into his lap, kissing me passionately as we melted into one another.

If we blocked out everything else that was going on, it felt good being who we used to be, even if it was for a moment.

After our lovemaking, we lay naked on the coolness of the tiled roof. Kayan had fallen asleep with one hand holding my arm, making sure I could not escape and reminding me how much I was loved, which I had started to question since he had chosen to stay in Iran. I watched my captor sleep; he was so peaceful. On his back were the imprints of the tiles, remnants of our lovemaking.

Later on that evening, when we let reality back in, Kayan shared everything he had found out after going from one government office to another. The outcome had no promise. Just hearing it took me back to that little man holding up his hand and his five pudgy fingers.

Kayan put his arm around my neck, kissing me on top of my head like he always did. "It'll be okay, we'll be okay."

It seemed those words had become his affirmation. *What does that mean?* I thought. *What does "okay" look like? Spending my days writing affirmations and eating pickled onions while watching our neighbors live their lives?*

If I had grown up with a limited mindset, maybe this situation could have been tolerable, but I had been raised in a "The sky's the limit" kind of environment and anything less felt like sandpaper on the heart. I missed life. I missed experiencing life as it opened up around me. I missed all the everyday things that I'd taken for granted, like seeing family and friends and sharing all the stories we had accumulated during the week. Most of all, I missed my freedom.

That night, in rebellion, while Kayan slept, I dressed myself in all black clothing, pulled my hair up into my black hoodie, and made my way down the stairs where all was dark and quiet. I ever so carefully opened the large teal gates just a bit to squeeze through. I hadn't noticed before, but they made a deep squeal when opened. I stood on the other side of the gates, looking down the alley in one direction, then the other, thinking, *Okay you've escaped. Now what? What is this great escape all about?*

My mind screamed, *Run!*

I picked a direction and started to walk. I had to be careful not to lose my way. The alley was completely dark due to the city's blackouts. There were no street signs or markers, only walls protecting the homes. I imagined myself getting lost, unable to find my way back, and being discovered when daylight finally arrived. But the thoughts didn't stop me; I kept walking. The freedom and exercise felt so good—so much so that I picked up my pace and found myself running faster than I had ever run in my life!

The euphoria only lasted seconds before I felt my shoe catching on a stone and found myself falling. Not a trip and fall, more like a being shot from a cannon, flying through the air, waiting for the impact kind of fall. I hit the ground, bounced once, and rolled along the stone pathway, finally stopping face-up, noticing the stars in the blackened sky. I lay there waiting while all my body parts, one by one, checked in, allowing me the moment I needed to assess the situation.

My entire body ached so much it was hard to tell from where. So, I stayed still until I heard what sounded like footsteps and pulled myself to my feet. I looked for the source of the footsteps, not wanting to go in that direction, but it was so dark I couldn't see anything. I turned and headed back towards what I thought was the house. Because of all the tumbling, I wasn't sure which direction to go in. The voices got closer and then, from around a corner, several men appeared, walking towards me. I immediately lowered my head and turned my face away; I could hear them greet me as they passed.

I was limping now and limped faster. What I hadn't realized was during the fall my hood had uncovered my head and my long hair was standing up as if I had been electrified from catapulting through the air. The men seemed to stop and talk amongst themselves. I limped faster, pulling up my hood and tucking the wildness on my head back inside. One of them yelled in my direction; the others joined in yelling at me. I moved faster, unable to run with my broken body.

"Where's that damn gate?" I mumbled to myself. Where was that gate that I hated, the gate that kept me locked in and the rest of the world out? Did I make a wrong turn? I wanted to cry but took a few deep breaths instead, which made the pain coming from my legs lessen.

The men had caught up to me, which wasn't hard to do. Oh, who was I kidding? I was never a fast mover, and this moment was no different. A male voice speaking Persian whispered in my ear. One of the men tugged at my hood, pulling it off my head. "American?"

I swung my arms in their direction the way you would if a bug was threatening to bite you. They laughed, and then I heard it: the low squeal from the teal gates.

"Lara, are you out here?" Kayan was standing, half-asleep, in front of the gate.

I ran into his arms, the tears now streaming down my face. "I'm so sorry. I just wanted to go outside!"

By now the men following me had disappeared into the darkness of the night.

Kayan pulled my face towards him. "Are you crazy?"

"Yes, yes, I am, for God's sake. I'm watching strangers doing their laundry all day, scared that someone might discover me. Yes, I'm crazy!"

He pulled me closer to him. "I'm so, so sorry, Lara, this is all my fault."

We entered the safety of the courtyard. "Are you limping?" he asked.

"I just tripped, that's all," I said as drops of blood splatted on the white tile in the courtyard.

"Oh my God, you're bleeding!"

Kayan's mother called out to him. She was standing in the shadows. Whatever her words were, she was upset and her voice began to shrill.

Kayan yelled back at her, signaling her to go, which she didn't. Instead, she carried on in a mix between a cry and a chant. He helped me up the stairs to our room and took off my clothes, examining the damage from my fall. My body looked like a patchwork quilt of many colors, different shades of blue and red with touches of brown from the dirt I had picked up along the way.

That night Kayan became doctor, nurse, psychologist, and loving husband. Each one took a turn at trying to put my pieces back together. It was sleep that finally came and took the hurt away... while Kayan held my hand.

XXI

THE DEBT

The next morning, I woke up hearing Kayan and his mother in a heated discussion downstairs. I lay in bed trying to figure out what was being said, but more importantly, who was winning the argument. There was a sudden silence and Kayan busted into our room.

"Come on, Lara, let's get dressed. We're going out!"

I rolled over and found every point of pain my body had experienced, releasing the agony with a loud moan.

"Oh, Lara, this is not good." Kayan stood over me looking at my legs as he pulled back the rest of the covers.

"We're going out?" I asked. I sat up, ignoring the condition of my body. Kayan sat down next to me, massaging the parts of my legs that had not changed colors.

"Is it safe, Kayan?"

"You're not going to like this part, but my mother is going with us."

I lay back down, feeling the emotion start to well up inside. He brushed away the hair from my face.

"We're going to ask for help from a special Parliament that has been set up to help people who have lost family during the war."

I sat up again. "Do you really think they can do something, Kayan?"

"I don't know, but it's a chance we didn't have yesterday. My mom wants to go since my brothers were her sons."

I looked at the pictures of Kayan's brothers sitting on the table, acknowledging that this opportunity was due to their deaths. I silently thanked them. Kayan reached down to pull me to my feet. The pain was excruciating. My body felt like it was on fire as I hobbled.

"Maybe we should go another time when you're up to it?" he asked.

I immediately perked up and started throwing my clothes on. "I'm fine. Just a little stiff is all." There was no way I was going to miss an opportunity to leave Iran! I pulled myself together quickly, throwing on the chador.

It was awkward walking down the alley and getting into a taxi with Kayan's mother. Nothing was said between any of us. It was just as hard for Kayan to ask his mother for help, but I was sure she would have done almost anything to get rid of the one thing that might cause her to lose her son.

Kayan opened the front passenger door for his mother to sit, and the two of us climbed in the back. He held my hand in a way that made it feel like it was a secret. It felt like something kids do to hide their feelings for each other from adults, like he was breaking a trust between his mother and him. Somehow, I had become the third wheel, but maybe I had always been. Whatever it was, it felt ugly, as if holding his wife's hand was a betrayal to his mother.

I took my hand back and through the window watched the city start to come alive. It was early morning and there were already lines in front of most businesses. Kayan had told me before that since the war supplies were being rationed, every family received books with vouchers that could be used to buy things like bread, milk, and other items. There were also vouchers for gas and oil. Since everything was in limited supply, vouchers were being traded on the black market. But the lines were most likely caused by people bartering. You didn't simply buy milk and eggs in Iran; you argued to get the best deal, and that took time. It was a cultural norm. Way before the war, people seemed to take pleasure in getting a better price for a package of flat bread. It was expected even if it was the same package of bread you bought every morning.

The taxi pulled up to a very tall, official-looking building with the usual pictures and flyers of Khomeini plastered all over it. People hustled about with a driving force. The majority were men dressed in suits and seemingly officious.

Kayan's mother led the way with her son. He cleared a path for her as she walked, like you would for the Queen of England—yet another dynamic to this family. Kayan was so different with her than he was with me. When she was around it was as if he had this secret person hidden inside that he was careful not to let out.

I only knew the secret Kayan, and I adored him. Seeing this other person show up in his place was startling, but I understood the fear. This woman wielded power and guilt like a machete, taking down anyone or anything that crossed her. Now that I thought about it, she was the perfect person to get me out of the country.

An elevator took us to the fourth floor. I began noting things around me just in case I needed an escape plan. It sounded silly, but it wasn't. There was nothing silly or unreal about staying aware of my safety in Iran. So, I memorized our way. Fourth floor, first left, glass door with gold Persian writing. It turned out that all of the doors had gold Persian writing. I made a point of noting a small piece of molding that was missing from the door frame. Mental notes were my breadcrumbs.

Kayan opened the door for his mother. Her chador made an ominous whooshing sound as she entered. I cautiously followed, not wanting to feel the sharpness of her tongue nor blade of disapproval. Kayan moved in front of us, addressing the receptionist, who was a small, neat, tidy woman sitting behind an equally small secretary desk and wearing a black silk hijab. He spoke to the woman with his polite inside voice. I watched her reaction to him; she barely looked up. That was a mistake. Kayan's mother pushed her way in front of him, her voice cracking with emotion.

Unnerved by whatever Kayan's mother had said, the woman quickly jotted down the last name "Batmanglij" before getting up and walking through the door directly behind her. She was the gatekeeper.

We all took seats in the empty waiting room, Kayan sitting in the middle. Other than the noise coming from the outside hall, it was silent. I opened my purse and glanced at my passport, which I had hidden. My biggest fear was that someone would take it from me, so I'd had the idea to tuck it into a sock and bury it in my purse.

"Batmanglij!" The receptionist stood behind us and spoke loudly, as if the room was packed with people demanding her time. Kayan nervously jumped up, helping his mother out of her chair. I followed like the obedient wife. We were led to an office where a man dressed in a suit and tie sat behind a desk. He did not look up or acknowledge our presence in any way. His mistake.

First up was Kayan, who, in his indoor voice, began to explain our dilemma. The man listened politely. I was able to understand maybe a word or two from each sentence. The man had little to no reaction to what was being said. Ours was just another story to him. Again, his mistake. I wanted to speak up, but before I could, Kayan's mother burst into tears and pulled out of her purse two pictures of her deceased sons. She placed them on his desk just inches from his face. I thought, *Ahh, the swift swing of the machete making a clean cut.* The innocent man was visibly shaken. His face went pale and he looked to Kayan for help, but none was offered. Instead, Kayan went into detail about our situation, further entrapping the man in our story.

While others took over for me, I had to sit ever so quietly. It was frustrating and went against everything I was. It wasn't the language barrier, as many Persians spoke at least some English. It was the fact that I was a woman, and for that I had to take my place quietly in the background, just like I had at the restaurant.

The man sat unbelievably still in his chair, not saying a word. The story had been told, but he had no response. I couldn't let my only opportunity to leave Iran disappear without doing something.

"Please" was the only word that came out of my mouth. The man's attention shifted to me, his eyes looking over his glasses.

"Please," I repeated, and this time he gave a long sigh, removed his glasses, and tapped them on his desk repeatedly.

It was obvious he did not want to deal with me, and definitely not with Kayan's mother. Kayan started to speak quickly in an effort to gain the man's momentary attention. In a frustrated move, the man held his hand up in front of Kayan. My heart sank. It looked like we were about to be asked to leave the office of the only person who could maybe help me leave Iran.

But instead, the man reached for a blank piece of paper on his desk and quickly wrote down the name and address of someone who might be able to do something. He made the note official by stamping it with a large metal stamp and his signature. We were instructed to give that piece of paper to the person whose name he had written on it.

That someone happened to be the Prime Minister of Iran. Maybe it was just something to get us out of his office, but it felt good to be hopeful. The man stood and lowered his head in a respectful way. As we walked toward the door, I could see his relief and the color returning to his face.

When we got back to Kayan's home, Tala and Ahmed greeted us. They excitedly started to run off a list of questions, ending with, "Can they help you?"

Kayan's mother disappeared, and while Kayan answered the questions, I too listened, hanging on every repeated word that the man had said to Kayan and taking from the conversation that there was hope!

I noticed I had begun to detach from Kayan, and I didn't exactly understand the reasons why. Maybe it was anger or resentment. Maybe I wanted him to be someone he wasn't. Maybe I wanted him to face the guilt his mother had laid on him. Or maybe it was all of that. Mostly I think I was preparing myself to live a life without him, something that had been unimaginable just weeks before. Thinking the thought actually took my breath away, so I buried it.

Early the next morning we did a repeat of the day before, only this time we set out to find the Prime Minister of Iran.

The Prime Minister's office was a bit more luxurious; the building was much larger. There was more polished marble, and the nameplates on the doors of the individual offices were in shiny gold metal letters. There was also a big military presence at every door. They immediately took note of me and stepped in front of us. Kayan moved closer, putting his hand on the small of my back and letting them know I was with him. His mother spoke up and firmly ordered Kayan to show them the piece of paper we had been given. They examined it, handed it back to Kayan, and immediately backed down. It was a good feeling to know that whatever was written on that piece of paper had some sort of authority, so much so that the soldier escorted us to the Prime Minister's office on the tenth floor.

We took the first right and walked through two huge, solid dark wood doors guarded by armed soldiers standing on either side. Kayan handed the piece of paper to a receptionist clad in a black chador with a pen that seemed to be permanently attached to her hand. With her free hand, she took and read the note, her eyes glancing up first at me, then Kayan, and next his mother. She was noticeably annoyed and pointed with her pen toward several chairs for us to sit in. This woman demanded control, and we gave it to her!

We quietly sat for one hour, then two. Not one of us said a word during those two hours, and not one other person entered the office. I began to wonder if the Prime Minister was even there or if he existed at all. Or was he like the Wizard of Oz, hiding behind a curtain and pretending to be something he wasn't, and the receptionist the keeper of his secret?

"Do you know..." I started to ask the receptionist when Kayan nudged me with his elbow. I had broken the rules and spoken up for myself. She gave me the annoyed glare that she wore so well. I wouldn't have cared if the stakes weren't so high. I smiled back at her and said nothing else.

A few moments later she stood up, opened an office door behind her, and motioned silently for us to enter. She never said a word, just led us down a hallway to another office where a man sat behind a desk looking more like a prop than a working employee. Ah, the Wizard. He stood up and shook all our hands before motioning to three chairs patiently waiting for us. He seemed so unassuming, it was hard to believe he was the Prime Minister of anything.

My hopes were a bit diminished. I'd had visions of a strong, powerful figure that demanded respect. Instead, we sat across from a man who jumped when my mother-in-law spoke. Kayan was up first, telling the same story and motioning to me at the proper moments like I was a visual aid. Before this poor man could absorb what was being said, out came the two pictures from my mother-in-law's purse, which she strategically placed in front of him. As if on cue, she began crying and mumbling through her tears. Oh, the poor guy never had a shot. We were well rehearsed now. The goal was clear, and he was no match for my mother-in-law. She had lost two of her sons and she wanted the debt paid! What she really wanted was the threat of losing another son gone.

The Prime Minister sat back in his high-back office chair and swayed from side to side. He read the note that Kayan had handed him, then looked at me and said, "Passport?"

I looked at Kayan, not sure what to do. Losing my passport meant losing who I was. I would belong no-where. Yet here I was in front of the Prime Minister of Iran, seemingly my only chance at leaving the country. I dug through my purse and pulled out the sock con-taining my passport—not very dignified, but it served its purpose. I stood up and handed it to him. Kayan gave me a supportive smile, acknowledging the risk I was taking.

The Prime Minister thumbed through my passport. It seemed like an eternity. *Go ahead and just take it if that's what you're going to do*, I thought. He opened the passport to a blank page, leaned to one side of his desk, and out of a drawer he retrieved an even more impressive metal stamp than the one the man from the day before used.

He held it over my passport, banged it down once in the middle of the page, and finished it off with his signature.

"You have three days to leave the country. After that, you are on your own, and I cannot help you."

I stood up and gratefully accepted my passport from him. He looked into my eyes, which began to fill like small pools, tears spilling down my face and onto his desk. I thanked him again and turned to leave. Kayan and his mother shook the Prime Minister's hand. I could tell he just wanted us to go away.

The Prime Minister called out something in Persian. We turned back and saw him motioning to the pictures of the brothers still sitting on his desk. Kayan rushed back and collected them, apologizing as we all left the room.

I was going home. I looked at the pictures of Ali and Sergis tucked under Kayan's arm. It was bittersweet knowing the reason I was going home was a debt being paid for the deaths of these two young men defending their country. I don't think anything could ever come close to paying off that kind of debt.

THE LETTERS

When we got back to the house, Kayan and I immediately went to our room to discuss my leaving. There was not a lot of time. It would take two to three days by bus to get to the Turkish border, and that was if the bus didn't break down or get rerouted because of the war. So most likely we'd have to get someone to drive us. Kayan would go with me as far as the border, but from there I would be on my own to cross into Turkey and get to Istanbul. My valuable passport would get me back into the States.

The idea of physically sneaking across the Turkish border terrified me. What if I went the wrong way, or even worse, crossed paths with the wrong person? I knew it was only by the grace of God that I had made it through Turkey before, and this time I'd be alone.

The only other choice was to fly out of Iran and into Turkey. It was a huge risk. There was only one flight a week, and that would be tomorrow.

We had already experienced the insanity of the airport, and the chances of getting on a plane were not in my favor. If I made that choice and didn't get on a plane, it would be too late for me to cross the Turkish border. I replayed the image of that little man holding up his hand, showing me five fingers.

Kayan and I bounced ideas, thoughts, and fears back and forth, but in the end the decision was mine to make. I flashed back to being on that train with the men who had come for the American woman. I would never be able to shake the image of those two huge figures with swords tied at their waists standing over me, and this time I wouldn't have my guardian angel Cyrus.

"Lara, are you okay?" Kayan's words snapped me out of my thoughts.

"I'll take my chances at the airport," I answered.

And that was the plan we put into action.

I began packing and ran up to the roof to collect my notebook. I immediately saw the neighbor and dropped down to the ground. There was something different about her. I watched while she hung up a pink baby nightdress and diapers on the line. She'd had her baby. It was a girl!

I got so excited. I didn't even know this woman, and two days ago I'd feared her, yet seeing the tiny outfit made me almost giddy. *Stay down!* I told myself. *She mustn't see you.* But I ignored my own warning and jumped up, getting the woman's attention. I pointed to the baby's garment and crossed my hands over my heart. She smiled and crossed her hands over her heart. I waved goodbye, and she responded by doing the same. She was my friend, even if she was one of Khomeini's spies.

That night while Kayan was gone and I was busy repacking my suitcase and feeding our pet goldfish for the last time, making sure it would have a chance at life, Tala came up to our room. She was like a kitten that didn't want to leave your side. There was a sadness leaving a bright young woman like her in this male-dominated society. I hoped she would be strong enough and not married off as a cultural norm.

"One day I will come to the United States to see you, Lara," Tala shared.

I stopped what I was doing and looked at the sweet innocence that she was. "I would like that, Tala."

"Look, I'm ready to go," she said, opening the bottom drawer of the armoire and pulling out a passport with her name and picture on it. She handed it to me. "I'm ready!"

"Yes, you are." I placed my hand on her cheek. "You take care of this. It can take you anywhere in the world," I said and went to place it back in the cabinet.

Pulling out the drawer, I noticed it was stuffed with light blue overseas letters like the ones I had sent to Kayan, one for every day he was gone. I pulled a handful out of the drawer, examining them. They were all addressed to him and sent from me. They were also unopened.

"Where did these come from, Tala?"

She looked at me with wide-eyed innocence and shrugged. "Ma gets them in the mail and keeps them in the drawer."

I lifted the hundreds of letters with my hands, remembering a time when each one had been a lifeline to Kayan, so full of all the emotions and feelings of not knowing if he was alive or dead. I scooped them up and held them to my heart. Kayan and I had assumed the government had confiscated the letters when he didn't receive them. It was easier than letting yourself think the other person had stopped loving you.

Kayan entered the room. I quickly put the letters back and shut the cabinet drawer. I don't know why I didn't take them all out and show him what his mother had done. I think it was because I was digesting it myself.

"What are you two up to?" Kayan asked.

"Tala was showing me her passport," I answered.

"I told Lara I want to see her in the United States," Tala said, stumbling over her words, excited by the thought of going to America. She hugged me tightly. "I love you, Lara." Tears flowed from all three of us.

Ahmed entered the room. "No!" he exclaimed at the showing of affection. I grabbed him and pulled him in for a hug. I could feel his heart beat faster. Kayan started to cry and turned away, not wanting to look weak in front of his younger brother and sister.

"Okay, now go. I love you both. Study hard and grow up to do great things!" I told them.

Kayan opened the door, not giving them an option to stay. Shutting it behind them, he turned back to me, grabbed me in his arms, and lifted me off the ground.

"I don't want to lose you; I love you so much, Lara!"

We both cried, hyperventilating sobs, holding one another. I didn't speak; there were no words that would make anything any different than what it was. Our love was clear. The situation was beyond anything we could have ever anticipated. I knew we had both struggled with what we might have done differently, but in the end nothing would change, so nothing needed to be said.

For the rest of the night, we loved each other in the moment. Our lovemaking was not our usual playful expression. I wanted to absorb all our tenderness for a lifetime.

Very early the next morning, Kayan took my suitcase down the stairs.

"Wait, I forgot something!" I said.

I ran back into the room that Kayan and I had shared. I ran to the armoire, opened the drawer that contained all the letters I had sent him, and placed the letters on the table where the pictures of his brothers sat. I wanted him to never question how much he was loved. I looked back at that room one more time, wrapped the chador around my head, and closed the door behind me.

Kayan and I snuck out into the darkness of the early morning. We knew there were challenges ahead, the biggest one being whether I would be able to get on the plane. Oh, how I prayed I would never have to return to that house. I wouldn't let my mind take me there.

I kept affirming, *I will get on that plane today and leave Iran*, over and over again, leaving no space for any of the scary thoughts that kept trying to come in.

XXIII

SHINY ALUMINUM STAIRS

The streets of Tehran were still sleeping. One of the challenges was finding a taxi at this time of the morning. I took my position of hiding in the shadows so as not to scare drivers away. I was hoping the dark skies would give me the cover I needed, and it did. Kayan was able to flag down a small, empty European car that could barely fit my suitcase in the trunk. He and the taxi driver were determined to make it work, and their efforts paid off.

Kayan and I squeezed into the back. He explained where we were going and the driver confidently nodded back, allowing us to breathe a sigh of relief for the hour-long drive that we knew was ahead of us.

"What will you do when you get home?" Kayan asked, attempting casual conversation.

I hadn't even thought about what my life was going to be without him. I had lived without Kayan for over a year, waiting for him to come home. In my mind and heart, he was always with me, but this time he wasn't coming home, and I wished he hadn't asked me that question.

"I have no idea," I answered. "What about you?"

Emotion welled up in my throat. I really didn't want to know what he would do when I was gone and only asked to be socially correct, although I knew there was no correct way to be at a time like this.

Kayan turned and looked out the window. "Nothing. Think of you, think of us." He turned back to me and spoke softly, as if sharing a secret. "I wish I was going with you."

I looked up at him, shocked to hear him say those words. "What?" I asked.

"Nothing," he responded.

After Kayan's mother told him it would be the death of her if he were to leave, Kayan had never expressed wanting to come home to the States. It was hurtful and difficult to watch the one I loved, my husband, choose his mother over me. Hearing those words come from him now was both heartbreaking and healing. For whatever reason, even if it was guilt, he was choosing to stay in his country. I rested my head on his shoulder the rest of the way, holding back an avalanche of hurt.

We arrived at the airport, which was already busy and chaotic. Cars were parked everywhere, people seemingly lost as they walked in front of our car with what looked to be everything they owned. Sad, really. Kayan tapped our driver on the shoulder and motioned for him to pull over, which he did. In the middle of the street, we exited the taxi and retrieved my belongings from the trunk. After paying the driver, Kayan grabbed my hand and we took off running through the airport, which was not unusual. Hundreds of others were doing the same thing.

We would go in one direction and get directed to another area, only to be told we had been misdirected and have to go in another direction. Eventually, we reached the only airline ticket booth that was open, Iran Air. It was the only airline allowed to fly in or out of Iran. There was also an extraordinarily long line of people waiting. Luckily the plane wasn't taking off for hours, but by the time we did reach the counter, we had seen almost two of those hours pass.

Kayan looked at me and started to laugh.

"I'm glad to see you are enjoying yourself," I responded.

I was sitting in the middle of the airport, on my baby blue suitcase, tied up in the chador like a poorly wrapped package with my eyes popping out from the sides. I obviously had lost all concern for appearances.

He tried to hold back the laughter. "I'm sorry. You look so cute sitting there."

I tried unsuccessfully to keep from laughing myself, but at the same time I was grateful to have a memory that would make me smile. The ticket clerk called out to Kayan. We both quickly approached the clerk. Kayan spoke with urgency in his voice, filling in the details about the importance of my getting a ticket on that plane. The clerk seemed to listen and then matter-of-factly spoke to us in English.

"There are 84 passengers already on the waiting list." He handed me a piece of paper with the number 85 written in Persian and English.

"No, please," I begged. "I have to be on that plane!"

"Name?" the clerk asked.

"Lara Batmanglij. Look, here's my passport. The Prime Minister of Iran signed it right here!"

The clerk took my passport and examined it. Kayan stepped in, pointing to the signature of the Prime Minister. The clerk handed my passport back to Kayan. From behind the counter, he pulled out a large binder, slowly turned to a page, and repeated my name while writing it in the book accompanied by the number 85—his answer to our emergency.

For a while Kayan and the clerk argued back and forth before we were asked to step out of line. We had been defeated. Passengers around us started to line up for the security check before boarding the plane.

"I made the wrong choice; I should have chosen to cross the border into Turkey!" I shouted.

Kayan grabbed me by the shoulders. "You did the right thing, Lara. Don't beat yourself up. Look at what's going on here!"

He motioned around the airport, where hundreds of others with probably just as important reasons were fleeing Iran. Some were crying, arguing, or just patiently waiting to find out their fate. Most were carrying everything of value they owned, only to have to leave it stacked up against the airport wall—the pile had doubled in size since our last visit. We calmly moved out of the way so others could be helped. A huge silken banner of Khomeini hung against a wall. We watched while passengers moved through the security checkpoint.

"Lara, wait here and don't move!"

Before I could respond, Kayan had taken off running through the airport. The silk banner of Khomeini brushed against my face. I pushed it away, wanting to tear it down. I would have if I thought I wouldn't have been shot on the spot. I moved a few feet over. I was spent.

The idea of returning to that house was unfathomable. Waiting for Tala and Ahmed to hurry home to share their day, Kayan's mother lurking in the shadows of our lives, and the worst part, having Kayan feeling guilty every time he looked at me. The reality of my fate was sinking in.

Kayan ran up to me and grabbed my arm. "Lara, let's go!"

Before I could form a thought, he had picked up my suitcase and started running with me through the airport.

"Where are we going?" I asked.

He turned back and handed me a piece of paper with the number three written on it. "You're on, let's go!"

I could feel tears suddenly rolling down my face. I was both excited and sad. We ran through the airport to a separate line where only the two of us stood.

"Kayan, how, how did this happen?"

"It doesn't matter, you're on the plane and it leaves in minutes!"

Two women employees came and escorted me through security. They quickly patted me down, opening up my suitcase and backpack, searching through them like all the other times.

I looked for Kayan. I didn't get to say goodbye. *I can't just leave. I need to say goodbye!* I started to panic as the women pushed me through security and out onto the tarmac. An Iran Air airplane sat waiting with its shiny silver aluminum stairs attached. I looked back and saw Kayan pleading with the women in security to let him pass. I tried to go to him, but he waved me on. I couldn't move. One of the security officers stepped aside, letting him go.

I dropped my suitcase and ran to him, jumping into his arms. Kayan lifted me off the ground, holding and kissing me.

"I love you, Lara Anderson!"

"I love you, Kayan Batmanglij!"

The plane was loaded and waiting to go. Two of the security officers walked over, motioning for me to get onto the plane. I looked at those shiny stairs that beckoned me to them.

"Go, Lara. Hurry. I love you!"

I picked up my suitcase and started to walk towards the airplane. A steward approached me, acknowledging my emotional state. He took my suitcase and kindly started helping me up the stairs. I looked back. Kayan stood watching me. My heart was breaking. I wanted to run back down the stairs and make a different choice. The forward movement in my feet slowed. Images of what my life would be like in Iran flashed in front of me. I entered the plane.

I numbly looked down the aisle of the plane that was packed with passengers. Everyone looked at me. There seemed to be a sympathetic kindness in their stare. A stewardess approached and I was directed to an aisle seat. A man sat next to me by the window.

I could see Kayan still standing in the same spot where I had left him.

The man stood up, offering me his seat. I madly waved from the window, getting Kayan's attention. Seeing me, he held up his hand. I placed mine up against the window.

The plane pulled the shiny aluminum stairs away and started its engines. I watched while the security officers kindly escorted Kayan back inside the airport. The plane taxied, bouncing along the runway. The passengers erupted into cheers...

ONE YEAR LATER

It was another one of those amazingly beautiful days in Malibu. I wanted it that way. My fellow surfers acknowledged me as I walked to the water's edge and dropped my board into the shallow waves. My breathing was deeper than normal, and I understood why. I kept reminding myself to breathe as I made my way out into the silence of the calmer waters. *Deep breaths*, I told myself.

My mind was caught up in the memories of Kayan taking that ride with me, his trembling body up against my back. I let the board glide to a stop, remembering us playing in the water, holding one another. I remembered brushing his long, dark curls off of his face and his larger-than-life smile leaning in for a kiss.

I twisted my wedding ring around my finger, reflecting back to the day when he proposed, how he'd held out the ring nervously, trying not to drop it in the ocean while he waited for my answer. I slipped the ring off of my finger, looking at it like it was my best friend. Oh, the stories it held.

Then, ever so gently holding it in the palm of my hand, I lowered the ring into the water and released it. The sun reflected off the gold while it playfully bobbed back and forth in the water before descending out of my view.

I took a few more deep breaths before turning my board around, catching the smallest of waves to carry me back to shore...

EPILOGUE

"If you don't tell your story, you betray it."

—*Gandhi*

The war between Iran and Iraq lasted almost eight years. On August 21, 1988, with the help of the United Nations, Iran accepted Iraq's ceasefire. Over a million lives were lost between the two countries.

To this day, Iran remains under Islamic leadership. I never saw Kayan again. He reached out once in the hope of coming home to the States, but his mother intercepted my calls and any communication by mail.

Of course, life did go on. I remarried more than once and had two sons, but my love for Kayan remains. It's true what they say: love never dies. Not the real stuff, not for me. It sometimes shifts from here to there, demanding more attention than I want to give it, always hanging back and waiting for the opportunity to appear and make me feel those feelings again, whether I want to or not...

Reminding me of how much I miss Kayan. How much I miss us.

About the Author

Robin Peterson has been a writer of film and stories for over 30 years. She is often referred to as the writer of 180 degrees, searching and looking for stories from all walks of life.

Always looking for the story that makes herself and her readers feel.

Ms. Peterson has raised two sons. Was a foster parent, an adoptive parent and later an adoptions ambassador for the City of Los Angeles.

She has also run and operated her own successful real estate business for over 17 years.

Passionate about writing and reading she recently started a reader's resource, Rpetersonbooks.com.

Satan Has Blue Eyes, is an intimate story that has taken the author almost 36 years to tell and is shared with the feeling and emotion as if it were today.

Robin Peterson currently lives in Southern California with her husband.